ITALIAN
ONE STEP AT A TIME

ITALIAN
ONE STEP AT A TIME

THE ULTIMATE STEP-BY-STEP COOKBOOK

LAURA ZAVAN

PHOTOGRAPHY BY PIERRE JAVELLE

＊ ＊ ＊

hamlyn

First published in France in 2007 under the title
Les basiques italiens, by Hachette Livre (Marabout)
Copyright © 2007 Hachette Livre (Marabout)

© Text Laura Zavan
Photography by Pierre Javelle

An Hachette UK Company
www.hachette.co.uk

First published in Great Britain in 2009 by
Hamlyn, a division of Octopus Publishing Group Ltd
2–4 Heron Quays, London E14 4JP
www.octopusbooks.co.uk

Copyright © English edition
Octopus Publishing Group Ltd 2009

ISBN 978-0-600-61950-5

A CIP catalogue record for this book is available from the
British Library

Printed and bound in Singapore

10 9 8 7 6 5 4 3 2 1

Measurements Metric and imperial measurements
have been given in all recipes. Use one set of
measurements only and not a mixture of both.
Standard level spoon measurements are used in
all recipes.
1 tablespoon = one 15 ml spoon
1 teaspoon = one 5 ml spoon

Nuts This book includes dishes made with nuts and
nut derivatives. It is advisable for those with known
allergic reactions to nuts and nut derivatives and
those who may be potentially vulnerable to these
allergies, such as pregnant and nursing mothers,
invalids, the elderly, babies and children, to avoid
dishes made with nuts and nut oils. It is also advisable
to check the labels of preprepared ingredients for
the possible inclusion of nut derivatives.

Eggs should be large unless otherwise stated. The
Department of Health advises that eggs should not
be consumed raw. This book contains dishes made
with raw or lightly cooked eggs. It is advisable for
more vulnerable people, such as pregnant and nursing
mothers, invalids, the elderly, babies and young
children, to avoid uncooked or lightly cooked dishes
made with eggs. Once prepared these dishes should
be kept refrigerated and used promptly.

Milk should be full fat unless otherwise stated.

Butter is unsalted unless otherwise stated.

Fresh herbs should be used unless otherwise stated.
If unavailable use dried herbs as an alternative but
halve the quantities stated.

Ovens should be preheated to the specific
temperature – if using a fan-assisted oven, follow
manufacturer's instructions for adjusting the time
and the temperature.

FOREWORD

~~~~~~

With this book you will discover, one step at a time, that Italian cookery is the most simple, tasty and natural way of bringing food to the table that you could imagine… and one that is easily adapted to suit your requirements.

The recipes here include a selection that are really quick to prepare and cook, such as the grilled vegetables or pasta dishes, and others that you may have never dared to attempt, such as risotto or homemade pizza: no longer a mystery to you! You will enjoy some very special culinary moments, such as making your own lasagne or ravioli. Make them with friends for even more fun!

Italian cooking is founded on a simple philosophy: good ingredients. Think of a perfect tomato: its flavour, smell, texture, colour. Served with no more than a drizzle of extra virgin olive oil and some basil: it's a feast!

It may take a little more time to seek out really good ingredients but once you've tracked down a decent source, everything becomes easy!

So allow yourself to discover this sun-filled cuisine, so warm and convivial. I invite you to share, like me, a moment of happiness: cooking is like love, and it does us so much good.

Buon appetito!

Laura

✹ ✹ ✹

CONTENTS

1
STARTERS

2
VEGETABLES

3
PASTA & CO.

4
FISH

5
MEAT

6
DESSERTS

APPENDICES
GLOSSARY • MENUS • TABLE OF CONTENTS
RECIPE INDEX • GENERAL INDEX
ACKNOWLEDGEMENTS

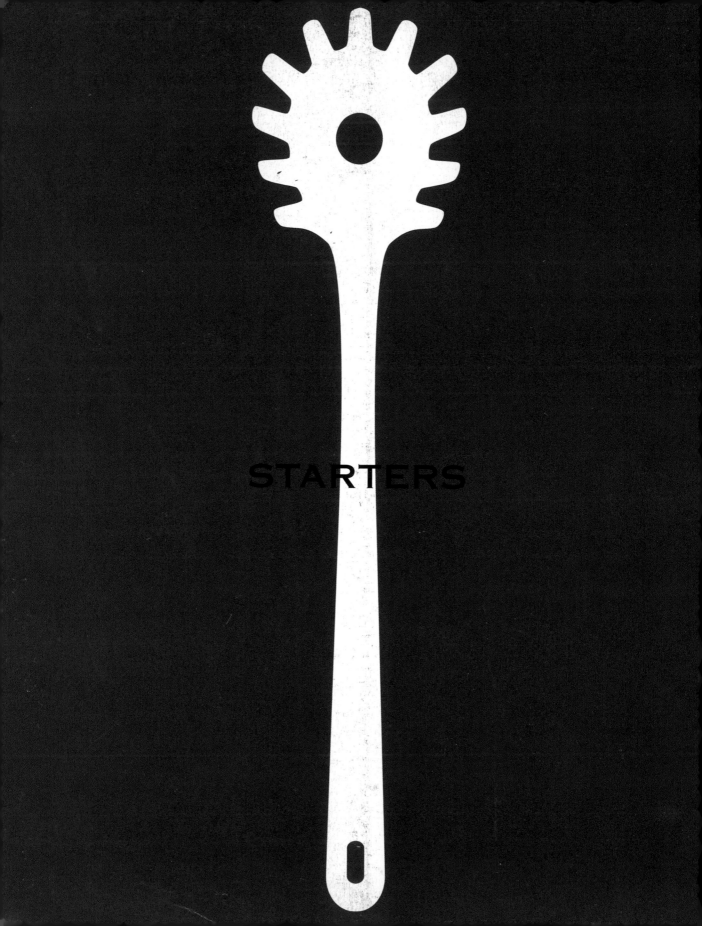

STARTERS

PESTOS

Classic pesto 01
Sicilian-style pesto 02
Pistachio pesto 03
Artichoke pesto 04

TOASTED

Bruschetta with tomato 05
Bruschetta toppings 06
Lingue 07
Breadsticks (grissini) 08
What to serve with lingue 09
What to serve with breadsticks 10

PIZZA & CO.

Focaccia with olives 11
Homemade pizza dough 12
Pizza margarita 13
Pizza toppings 14
Mini fried calzone 15

1

CLASSIC PESTO

❖ **SERVES 6** • PREPARATION: 15 MINUTES ❖

6–8 handfuls of basil leaves (100 g/3½ oz)
25 g (1 oz) pine nuts
15 g (½ oz) walnuts
1 garlic clove, peeled and crushed
salt flakes, pepper

25 g (1 oz) Parmesan, grated
100 ml (3½ fl oz) olive oil

IN ADVANCE:
Rinse and dry the basil leaves. Put the bowl of a food-processor, fitted with its blade, in the freezer for 1 hour. (This prevents the pesto from getting warm and losing its aromas.)

1 2
3 4

1	Dry-toast the pine nuts in a non-stick frying pan, stirring them constantly. Remove from the heat and allow to cool.	2	Put the basil in the chilled bowl with the toasted pine nuts, walnuts, crushed garlic and a pinch of salt and pepper.
3	Whiz for 30 seconds then add the grated Parmesan and the oil, pouring it in as a thin stream.	4	The pesto is ready! Spread on toasted bread slices with some mozzarella, or stir into pasta, diluted with a little of its cooking water.

SICILIAN-STYLE PESTO

❖ SERVES 6–8 • PREPARATION: 10 MINUTES ❖

Whiz together 40 g (1½ oz) of the following: pitted black olives, pitted green olives, salted capers (rinsed) and sun-dried tomatoes with 1 tablespoon dried oregano,

1 handful of basil leaves and 2 handfuls of flat leaf parsley. Pour in up to 100 ml (3½ fl oz) olive oil in a thin stream until the consistency is rich and smooth.

IDEAS:
Serve this pesto spread on toasted bread slices or stirred into pasta, diluted with a little of the pasta cooking water.

PISTACHIO PESTO

⇾ SERVES 8 • PREPARATION: 10 MINUTES ⇽

Toast 125 g (4 oz) raw shelled pistachios for 10 minutes at 160°C (325°F), Gas Mark 3. Allow to cool, then whiz with 3–4 handfuls of rocket leaves and 50 g (2 oz) of freshly grated Pecorino romano. Pour in up to 150 ml (5 fl oz) olive oil in a thin stream until you have a smooth paste. Season with salt, pepper and grated nutmeg.

IDEAS:
Serve this pesto spread on toasted bread slices, mixed with ricotta, or over pasta, or to accompany pan-fried or roasted meat.

ARTICHOKE PESTO

❧ **SERVES 6–8** • **PREPARATION: 30 MINUTES** ❧

25 g (1 oz) almonds, skinned
75 ml (3 fl oz) olive oil
2 garlic cloves, peeled
1 handful of flat leaf parsley

8 artichoke hearts, fresh or frozen
salt
40 g (1½ oz) freshly grated Parmesan

IN ADVANCE:
Lightly dry-toast the almonds in a frying pan then roughly chop them.

1	Heat 2 tablespoons of the olive oil in a frying pan with 1 garlic clove and half the parsley.	2	Add the artichoke hearts and brown on both sides over a high heat. Add salt and 50 ml (2 fl oz) water, cover and simmer for 10 minutes.
3	Drain, allow the hearts to cool, then blend with the remaining garlic clove and parsley and the Parmesan and pour in enough oil in a thin stream to make a smooth rich mixture.	4	It's ready! Serve the pesto spread on toasted bread slices or as an accompaniment to white meats.

BRUSCHETTA WITH TOMATO

⇻ SERVES 4 · PREPARATION: 20 MINUTES · RESTING: 1 HOUR ⇺

1 bunch of basil
750 g (1½ lb) just-ripe plum tomatoes
100 ml (3½ fl oz) olive oil
3–4 garlic cloves, peeled, salt + pepper
8–10 slices of good-quality country-style
bread, about 1-cm (½-in) thick

IN ADVANCE:
Roughly chop the basil leaves. Skin the
tomatoes (pierce with a knife then plunge
in boiling water for 30 seconds and the
skins will slip off easily).

VARIATIONS:
Instead of garlic on the bread, use anchovy
fillets, marinated or in oil, or slices of
buffalo mozzarella before topping with
the tomatoes.

1 2
3 4

1	Deseed the tomatoes and cut into small dice. Put them in a colander and sprinkle with salt (this removes the excess water and accentuates their flavour). Set aside for 30 minutes.	2	Tip the tomatoes into a bowl with the olive oil, 2–3 garlic cloves, sliced (remove them before serving) and the basil. Taste and season as required. Set aside for a further 30 minutes.
3	Toast the bread slices, rub a cut garlic clove lightly over the surface, season then drizzle with olive oil.	4	Top the bread slices with the diced marinated tomatoes and serve immediately.

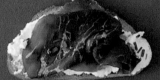

BRUSCHETTA TOPPINGS

MEAT	CHEESE
⤇ coppa (cured ham) + black olive tapenade	⤇ warm Gorgonzola, mascarpone + walnuts
⤇ lardo di Colonnata (cured pork fat), tomato + rosemary	⤇ Pecorino + dried figs
⤇ bresaola (air-dried salt beef), goats' cheese + chives	⤇ warm Taleggio + pan-fried courgettes
⤇ prosciutto di San Daniele + artichokes in oil	⤇ smoked Provola, tomato + rocket

BRUSCHETTA TOPPINGS

FISH OR SHELLFISH	VEGETABLES
⤺ Sicilian aubergines (see recipe 23) + steamed prawns ⤺ grilled peppers (see recipe 16), tuna + basil ⤺ tinned mackerel in oil + tomato gratin (see recipe 25)	⤺ grilled vegetables (see recipes 16, 17 and 18) ⤺ Botargo (salted grey mullet roe) marinated with celery stalks, lemon + olive oil ⤺ oven-baked vegetables (see recipe 27) + capers

LINGUE

❧ **MAKES 12** • PREPARATION: 30 MINUTES • COOKING: 10 MINUTES x 2 OR 4 BATCHES • RESTING: 2 HOURS ❧

5 g (¼ oz) fresh or ½ sachet dried
100–150 ml (3½–5 fl oz) tepid water
¼ teaspoon sugar + 1 pinch
250 g (8 oz) strong plain flour
½ teaspoon fine salt + olive oil

IN ADVANCE:
Prepare the dough as for pizza (see recipe 12)
but using the quantities listed here. Knead
the dough for 5 minutes then leave to prove
in a warm place, covered with a tea towel,

for 1 hour. Knock back, knead again then
leave to prove for a further 30 minutes.
Preheat the oven to 240°C (475°F),
Gas Mark 9. Prepare a selection of toppings
(see recipe 09 for some delicious ideas).

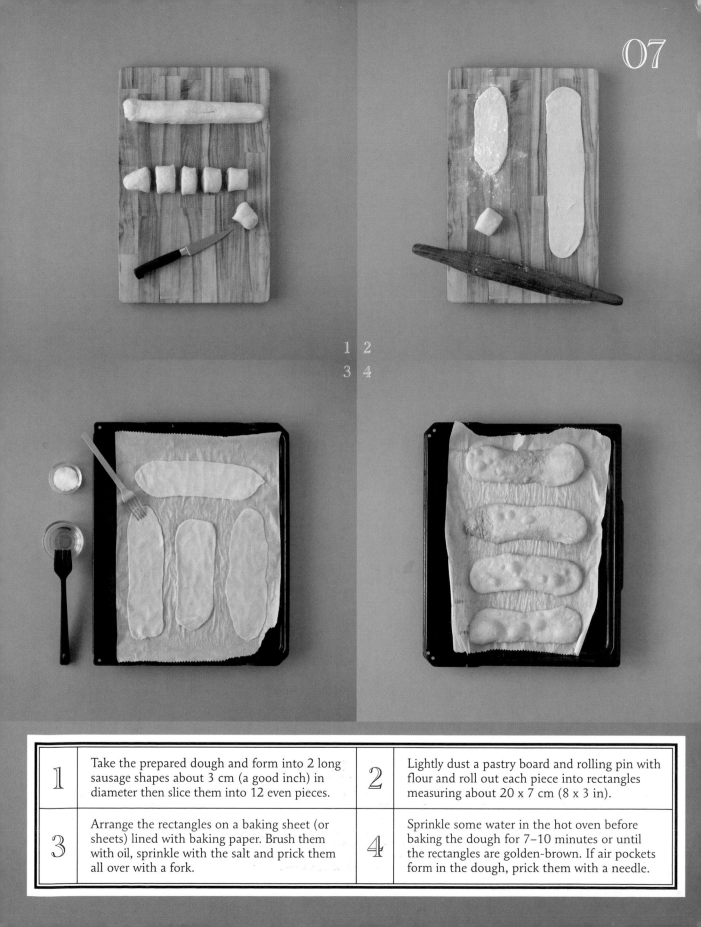

1	Take the prepared dough and form into 2 long sausage shapes about 3 cm (a good inch) in diameter then slice them into 12 even pieces.	2	Lightly dust a pastry board and rolling pin with flour and roll out each piece into rectangles measuring about 20 x 7 cm (8 x 3 in).
3	Arrange the rectangles on a baking sheet (or sheets) lined with baking paper. Brush them with oil, sprinkle with the salt and prick them all over with a fork.	4	Sprinkle some water in the hot oven before baking the dough for 7–10 minutes or until the rectangles are golden-brown. If air pockets form in the dough, prick them with a needle.

BREADSTICKS (GRISSINI)

MAKES 30 • PREPARATION: 40 MINUTES • RESTING: 1 HOUR 30 MINUTES • COOKING: 15 MINUTES

20 g (¾ oz) fresh or 2 sachets dried yeast
200–250 ml (7–8 fl oz) tepid water
½ teaspoon sugar + 1 pinch
500 g (1 lb) strong plain flour
1 teaspoon fine salt + 6 tablespoons olive oil

IN ADVANCE:
Prepare the dough as for pizza (see recipe 12) but using the quantities listed here. Divide the dough into three pieces. Knead a little dried oregano into the first,

1 tablespoon sesame seeds into the second, and 1 tablespoon chopped walnuts into the third. Leave to prove in a warm place, covered with a tea towel, for 1 hour.

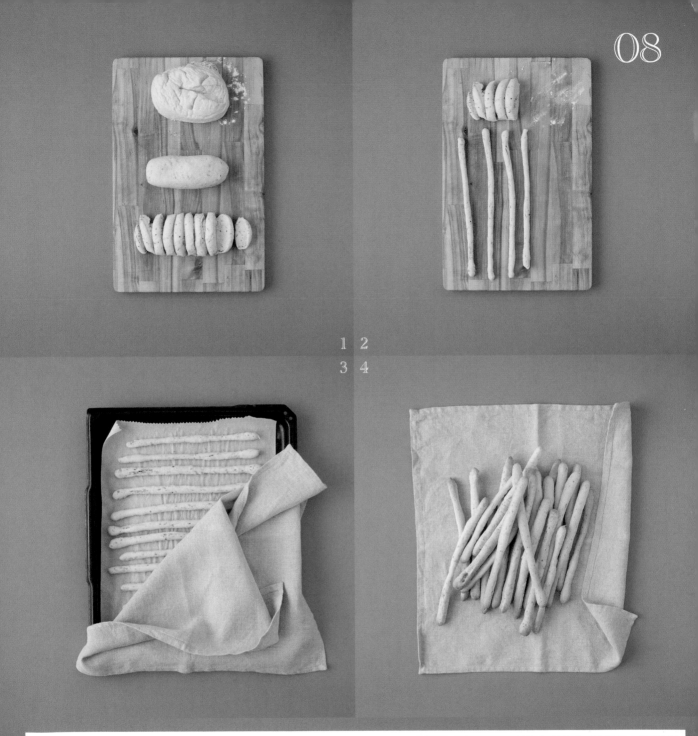

1	Lightly knead each piece of dough for 30 seconds, then form into a sausage shape and cut into about 10 slices.	2	Use your hands to roll out each slice into sticks about 1.5 cm (¾ in) thick and 10 cm (4 in) long.
3	Arrange the breadsticks on a baking sheet lined with baking paper. Leave to prove for a further 30 minutes, covered with a damp tea towel.	4	Preheat the oven to 200°C (400°F), Gas Mark 6 and cook the breadsticks for about 15 minutes. See recipe 10 for serving ideas.

WHAT TO SERVE WITH LINGUE

TIP: SPREAD ONLY AT THE LAST MINUTE, OR SERVE THE TOPPINGS AND THE LINGUE SEPARATELY.

✧ ⅔ ricotta blended with ⅓ dried tomatoes + basil
✧ ⅔ ricotta blended with ⅓ Pistachio Pesto (recipe 03)
✧ ⅔ Pistachio Pesto blended with ⅓ botargo + pimiento
✧ ⅔ ricotta blended with ⅓ Pesto (recipe 01) + pine nuts

✧ Sicilian-style Pesto (recipe 02) + basil
✧ ½ mascarpone blended with ½ anchovies + oregano
✧ Artichoke Pesto (recipe 04), parsley + almonds
✧ tapenade + Oven-baked Cherry Tomatoes (recipe 26)

WHAT TO SERVE WITH GRISSINI

TIP: PREPARE ONLY AT THE LAST MINUTE SO THAT THE BREADSTICKS DON'T SOFTEN.

⤙ Parma ham, mascarpone + rocket leaves
⤙ lardo di Colonnata (cured pork fat), cut very finely
⤙ bresaola, mascarpone, chives + lemon rind
⤙ cooked ham, artichokes in oil + mascarpone

⤙ coppa (cured ham), dried tomato purée + mascarpone
⤙ speck (cured mountain ham), butter + gherkins
⤙ Culatello di Zibello (speciality Parma ham), on its own
⤙ Mortadella, Pistachio Pesto + mascarpone

OLIVE FOCACCIA

SERVES 8 • PREPARATION: 30 MINUTES • RESTING: 2 HOURS 30 MINUTES • COOKING: 30 MINUTES

Pizza dough (see recipe 12) made with
350 ml (12 fl oz) water (it should be sticky)
100 g (3½ oz) pitted taggiascha olives
6 tablespoons olive oil
4 tablespoons tepid water
1 level tablespoon salt flakes

VARIATIONS:
Work into the dough 2 tablespoons
chopped rosemary leaves, 1 small handful
snipped fresh sage leaves, or 10 salted
anchovy fillets, rinsed and cut very small.

Just before transferring the dough to the
oven, top with either 100 g (3½ oz) halved
cherry tomatoes or 2 onions sliced finely
into rings.

1 2
3 4

1	Knead the dough, working in the olives, for 1 minute before spreading it out on an oiled baking sheet, pressing it with your hands from the centre towards the edge.	2	Use a fork to beat together the olive oil with the tepid water and the salt (it should dissolve a little).
3	Using your fingertips, make little dimples over the surface of the dough, brush over half the oil mixture and leave to rest for 30 minutes.	4	Preheat the oven to 180°C (350°F), Gas Mark 4 and cook for 30 minutes until the top is golden. Brush with the remaining oil mix.

HOMEMADE PIZZA DOUGH

❧ PREPARATION: 20 MINUTES • RESTING: 2 HOURS 20 MINUTES • COOKING: 20 MINUTES ❧

25 g (1 oz) fresh or 2 sachets of dried yeast
250–300 ml (8–10 fl oz) tepid water
½ teaspoon sugar + 1 pinch

500 g (1 lb) strong plain flour
1 teaspoon fine salt
3 tablespoons olive oil

1 2
3 4

1	Crumble the yeast. Add 3 tablespoons of the water and the pinch of sugar. Leave for 15 minutes to activate.	2	Sift the flour into a large mixing bowl, sprinkle with the salt around the edges then pour the yeast mixture into the centre.	
3	Stir in the sugar and oil, then gradually add in the remaining water.	4	Mix everything together using a fork.	➢

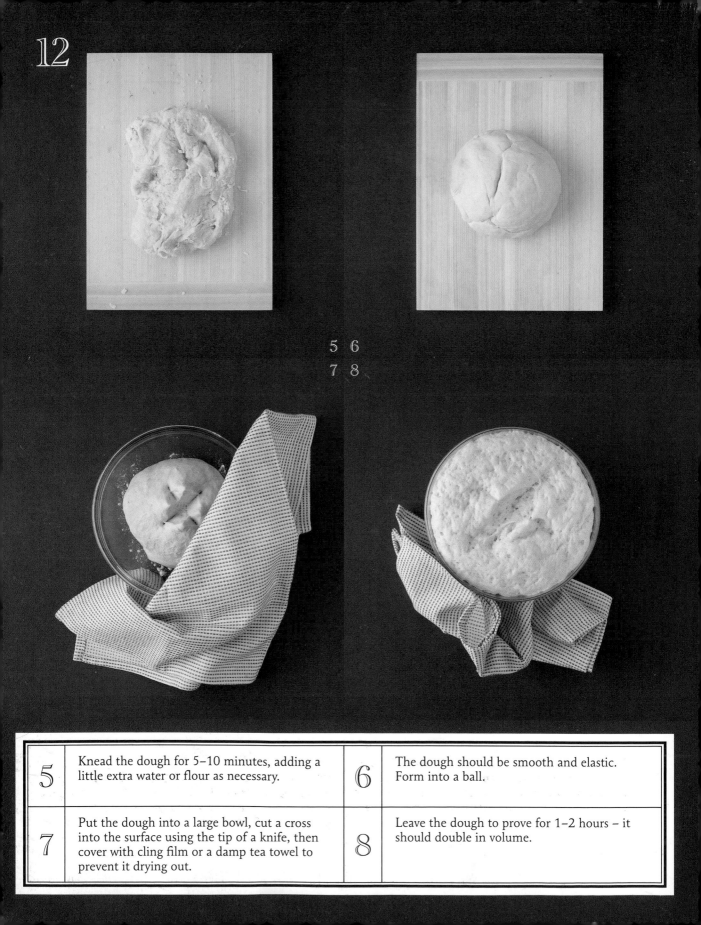

5 6
7 8

5	Knead the dough for 5–10 minutes, adding a little extra water or flour as necessary.	6	The dough should be smooth and elastic. Form into a ball.
7	Put the dough into a large bowl, cut a cross into the surface using the tip of a knife, then cover with cling film or a damp tea towel to prevent it drying out.	8	Leave the dough to prove for 1–2 hours – it should double in volume.

		TIP
9	Knock back and knead the dough for 1 minute then spread it out on an oiled baking sheet using your hands. For best results leave to prove again for a further 30 minutes, covered with a damp tea towel.	☛ For the yeast to work, the dough needs to rest in a warm place (25–30°C/77–86°F) away from draughts. Alternatively, place in an oven which has been preheated to 50°C (120°F) and then switched off.

PIZZA MARGARITA

❖ MAKES 10–14 SLICES • PREPARATION: 30 MINUTES • RESTING: 2 HOURS • COOKING: 20 MINUTES ❖

1 quantity Pizza Dough (see recipe 12)
250 g (8 oz) buffalo mozzarella (or, if you cannot find it, use a good mozzarella made from cow's milk)
400 g (14 oz) tin chopped tomatoes

1 garlic clove, peeled and crushed
1 tablespoon dried oregano
about 10 basil leaves
3 tablespoons olive oil
salt

IN ADVANCE:
Rework the dough for 1 minute before spreading it out with your hands on an oiled baking sheet. If possible, rest it for 30 minutes, covered with a damp tea towel.

1 2
3 4

1	Cut the mozzarella into small dice then leave it to drain.	2	Put the tomatoes with the crushed garlic in a bowl with the oregano, half the basil, cut or torn into pieces, and 2 tablespoons olive oil. Add salt and taste to check the seasoning.
3	Spread this mixture over the dough and drizzle with the oil. Bake at 240°C (475°F), Gas Mark 9. Add the mozzarella after 12 minutes.	4	Cook for a further 6 minutes. The crust and the top should be golden. Serve with the remaining basil cut or torn and scattered on top.

PIZZA TOPPINGS

TO PIZZA MARGARITA (SEE RECIPE 13) ADD ANY OF THE FOLLOWING TOPPINGS.

✦ **SALAMI:** once cooked, add some spicy salami.

✦ **AUBERGINES:** 5 minutes before the end of cooking add some aubergines, either roasted (see recipe 17) or pan-fried (see recipe 24), and sprinkle with Parmesan.

✦ **MEDITERRANEAN:** at the end, add 50 g (2 oz) each of capers and black olives. Sprinkle with dried oregano.

✦ **SUMMER:** at the end, add cherry tomatoes marinated with garlic, basil and olive oil, and some rocket leaves.

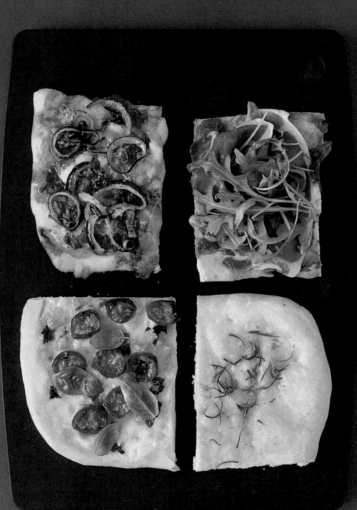

PIZZA TOPPINGS

TO PIZZA MARGARITA (SEE RECIPE 13) ADD ANY OF THE FOLLOWING TOPPINGS.

✦ **ONION & ANCHOVY:** add 6 anchovies, some sliced onion and olive oil before cooking.

✦ **'WHITE':** without tomato sauce. At the end, add cherry tomatoes, basil and olive oil.

✦ **PARMA HAM & ROCKET:** at the end, add some slices of Parma ham, rocket and a drizzle of olive oil.

✦ **'WHITE' WITH ROSEMARY AND OLIVE OIL:** drizzle with olive oil and sprinkle with rosemary before cooking.

MINI FRIED CALZONE

➤ **MAKES 16** • PREPARATION AND COOKING: 1 HOUR ◄

250 g (8 oz) mozzarella
about 10 basil leaves
1 quantity Pizza Dough (see recipe 12)
300 ml (10 fl oz) Tomato Sauce (see recipe 40)
vegetable or olive oil, for deep frying

IN ADVANCE:
Cut the mozzarella into small dice and leave
to drain. Roughly chop the basil.

IDEAS:
Add some chopped cured meats:
ham, salami, mortadella and so forth.

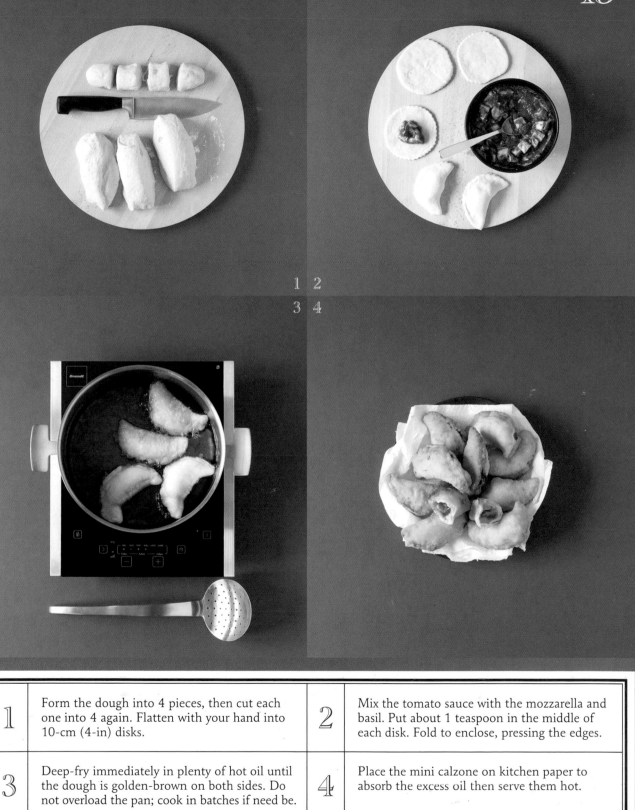

1	Form the dough into 4 pieces, then cut each one into 4 again. Flatten with your hand into 10-cm (4-in) disks.	2	Mix the tomato sauce with the mozzarella and basil. Put about 1 teaspoon in the middle of each disk. Fold to enclose, pressing the edges.
3	Deep-fry immediately in plenty of hot oil until the dough is golden-brown on both sides. Do not overload the pan; cook in batches if need be.	4	Place the mini calzone on kitchen paper to absorb the excess oil then serve them hot.

VEGETABLES

2

GRILLED VEGETABLES

Grilled peppers 16
Grilled aubergines 17
Grilled courgettes 18

SALADS

Orange & fennel salad 19
Bread salad (panzanella) 20
Raw artichoke salad 21

COOKED VEGETABLES

Stewed peppers (peperonata) 22
Sicilian aubergines (caponata) 23
Neapolitan-style aubergines 24
Tomato gratin 25
Oven-baked cherry tomatoes 26
Oven-baked vegetable medley 27

LIGHT DISHES

Courgette frittata 28
Herb & vegetable pie................................. 29
Minestrone 30
Borlotti bean soup 31

GRILLED PEPPERS

❧ **SERVES 4** • PREPARATION: 10 MINUTES • COOKING: 30 MINUTES • MARINATING: 1 HOUR ❧

4 peppers

FOR THE MARINADE:
olive oil
2–3 basil stalks (or other fresh herbs)
3 garlic cloves, thinly sliced
salt and freshly ground pepper

IN ADVANCE:
Preheat the grill to its maximum setting.

1 2
3 4

1	Cut the peppers in half from top to bottom and remove the seeds and membranes. Place them in a baking tray, cut side down, under the grill.	2	Watch them carefully: as soon as they develop dark patches, but without blackening completely, remove them from the grill.
3	Place the peppers in a large bowl, cover it with cling film and leave to cool. Slip off the skins.	4	Cut the peppers into long thin slices then add the olive oil, basil, garlic and some salt and pepper to the bowl. Marinate for 1 hour.

GRILLED AUBERGINES

❧ **SERVES 4** • PREPARATION: 10 MINUTES • COOKING: 20 MINUTES ❧

Cut 2 aubergines lengthways into slices around ½ cm (¼ in) thick. Spread the slices out on a baking sheet covered with baking paper, brush with olive oil and sprinkle with salt. Put under a very hot grill until the slices are golden-brown (watch them carefully to check they don't burn) then turn them over. Sprinkle with oregano and grill the slices until the second side is golden.

GRILLED COURGETTES

✦ **SERVES 4** • PREPARATION: 10 MINUTES • COOKING: 20 MINUTES ✦

Cut 3 courgettes lengthways into slices ½ cm (¼ in) thick. Spread them out in a baking tray covered with baking paper, brush with olive oil and sprinkle with salt. Put under a very hot grill until the slices are golden-brown (watch carefully to check they don't burn) then turn them over. Sprinkle with oregano and grill until the second side is golden.

☞ Dress the courgettes with vinegar, if liked.

ORANGE & FENNEL SALAD

❧ **SERVES 4** • **PREPARATION: 20 MINUTES** ❧

2 large oranges
2 fennel bulbs
150–200 g (5–7 oz) smoked swordfish
(optional)

1 red onion
65 g (2½ oz) green olives
6 tablespoons olive oil
salt and freshly ground pepper

DE-LUXE VARIATION:
Instead of swordfish, you can use shavings
of botargo.

1 2
3 4

1	Peel the oranges and cut them into pieces. Thinly slice the fennel and cut the swordfish (if using) into dice.	2	Slice the onion into rings and rinse in plenty of water to make the flavour less strong. Drain.
3	Combine the onion rings in a salad bowl with the oranges, fennel, swordfish and olives.	4	Drizzle in the olive oil, season with salt and pepper, and it's ready!

PANZANELLA

⇥ SERVES 4 • PREPARATION: 20 MINUTES • MARINATING: 1 HOUR ⇤

8 slices of stale country-style bread
250 ml (8 fl oz) water
100 ml (3½ fl oz) olive oil + extra to serve
4 tablespoons good-quality red wine vinegar
salt and freshly ground pepper
1 red onion

500 g (1 lb) cherry tomatoes
1 small cucumber, peeled and deseeded
2 celery stalks
100 g (3½ oz) pitted black olives
50 g (2 oz) salted capers, rinsed and chopped
1 bunch of basil

IN ADVANCE:
Put the bread slices in a salad bowl.

QUICK TIP:
If you don't have any stale bread, you can simply toast some fresh slices.

1   2   3
4   5   6

1	In a small bowl, mix together the water, olive oil, half the vinegar and some salt and pepper.	2	Pour this mixture over the bread and leave to swell. If there is not enough liquid, add a little extra water.	3	Cut the onion into rings and all the vegetables into even-sized dice. Transfer everything to a dish.
4	Add the olives, capers, basil, and the rest of the vinegar. Season with salt and pepper.	5	In a large salad bowl, layer alternately the soaked bread and the vegetables.	6	Leave to marinate for 1 hour. Drizzle with extra olive oil before serving.

RAW ARTICHOKE SALAD

➤ **SERVES 6** • PREPARATION: 15 MINUTES ➤

6 small purple artichokes (poivrades or Provence artichokes)
2 lemons
½ bunch of flat leaf parsley

6 tablespoons olive oil
salt flakes, freshly ground pepper
100 g (3½ oz) Parmesan shavings

SUGGESTION:
Serve with Carpaccio of Beef (see recipe 62) or with pan-fried Veal Escalopes (see recipe 65).

1 2
3 4

1	Use a sharp knife to remove the top 2 cm (5 in) of the artichokes and cut off their stalks. Remove the toughest outer leaves.	2	Put each prepared artichoke immediately into water acidulated with some lemon juice to prevent them from blackening.
3	Cut the artichokes into very thin slices. Chop the parsley.	4	Mix together the olive oil with 2 tablespoons of lemon juice and the parsley. Season with salt and pepper. Drizzle over the artichokes and serve immediately, topped with the Parmesan.

STEWED PEPPERS (PEPERONATA)

❖ SERVES 4 • PREPARATION: 15 MINUTES • COOKING: 35 MINUTES ❖

4 peppers (red, yellow, green)
4 ripe tomatoes, or use a tin of chopped
tomatoes
2 onions

2 garlic cloves, peeled
3 tablespoons olive oil
1 bunch of basil
salt and freshly ground pepper

SUGGESTION:
This quintessentially summer dish can be
served with chicken, tuna or rice dishes,
or spread on little toasts.

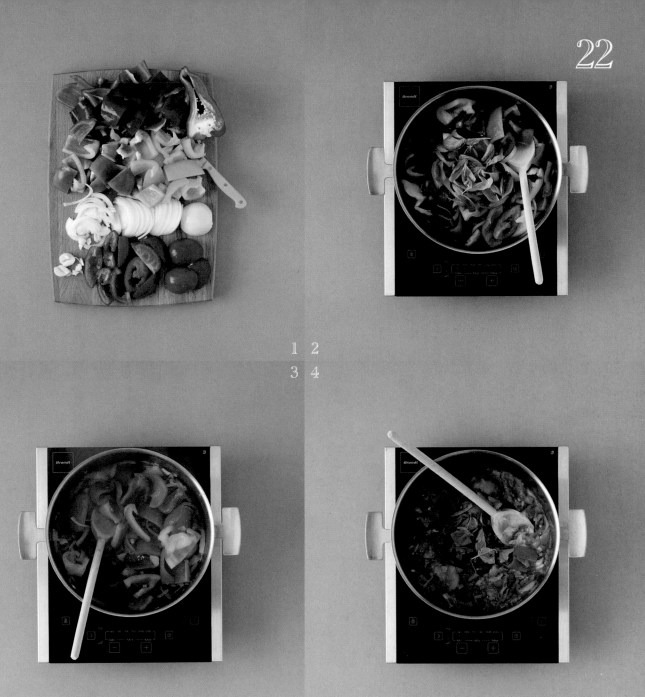

1	Deseed the peppers and cut into large chunks. Quarter and deseed the tomatoes. Finely chop the onions and the garlic.	2	Heat the oil in a saucepan and cook the onions for 2 minutes to soften. Add the tomatoes, peppers, garlic and half the basil leaves.
3	Cook over a high heat for 5 minutes, add salt then simmer, covered, for 20 minutes. Remove the lid and cook until the liquid has evaporated.	4	Roughly chop or tear the remaining basil leaves and stir in. Serve warm or at room temperature.

SICILIAN AUBERGINES (CAPONATA)

❖ **SERVES 4–6** • PREPARATION: 30 MINUTES • COOKING: 20 MINUTES ❖

3 plum tomatoes
3 aubergines
2 celery stalks + 2 small onions
olive oil, for frying
4 tablespoons pitted green olives

1 tablespoon raisins
2 tablespoons pine nuts
1 tablespoon salted capers, rinsed
2 tablespoons red wine vinegar
1 level tablespoon sugar

IN ADVANCE:
Pierce the skins of the tomatoes then plunge in boiling water for about 30 seconds. Refresh under running water and slip off the skins.

| 1 | Cut the aubergines into 2-cm (about 1-in) cubes. String the celery and cut into small pieces. Quarter and deseed the tomatoes and dice. Finely chop the onions. | 2 | Heat the olive oil in a frying pan and fry the aubergines, in batches, stirring frequently, until they are tender. (You may need to add extra oil to the pan between batches.) Season with salt. | |
| 3 | Drop the celery into boiling salted water for 2 minutes. Remove and drain. | 4 | Heat a little olive oil in another pan, add the chopped onions and cook for 2 minutes to soften. | ➤ |

<table>
<tr><td>5</td><td>Add the aubergines and the celery, then the olives, raisins, pine nuts, capers and, at the end, the tomatoes. Gently stir to mix and leave to cook gently for 3 minutes.</td><td>**NOTE**
❀

☞ This is a lighter version of the original Sicilian caponata, which is made with deep-fried aubergines.</td></tr>
</table>

			SUGGESTION
6	Mix together the vinegar and the sugar then pour into the frying pan and continue to cook gently for a few minutes.		Serve warm or at room temperature as a side dish, spread on bruschetta as a starter, or with a pasta salad or rice dish.

NEAPOLITAN-STYLE AUBERGINES

❧ SERVES 4–6 • PREPARATION: 30 MINUTES • COOKING: 25 MINUTES ❧

2 aubergines
50 g (2 oz) Parmesan
125 g (4 oz) mozzarella

1 bunch of basil
vegetable or olive oil, for deep frying
salt
200 g (7 fl oz) Tomato Sauce (see recipe 40)

TIP:
Have ready a good supply of kitchen paper
to absorb the excess oil from the aubergines.

1	Slice the aubergines thinly across their width.	2	Grate the Parmesan and chop the mozzarella and the basil leaves.
3	Heat the oil in a heavy-based, deep-sided casserole. Fry the aubergines in batches to avoid overcrowding the pan.	4	As soon as the slices are golden-brown, spread them on kitchen paper to absorb all the oil. Sprinkle lightly with salt. ➤

5

Grease a medium gratin dish and cover the base with a layer of aubergine slices. Top with some of the tomato sauce, then sprinkle with chopped mozzarella and basil and grated Parmesan. Repeat the layers until you have used all the ingredients.

VARIATION
❋

☛ For a lighter version of this classic Neapolitan dish, 'melanzane alla parmigiana', you can grill the aubergine slices instead (see recipe 17).

		SERVING IDEAS
6	Transfer to a preheated oven at 180°C (350°F), Gas Mark 4 for about 5 minutes until the top is browned and bubbling.	Serve warm or at room temperature as a starter, with a rocket salad, with rice, or as a side dish.

TOMATO GRATIN

⇒ SERVES 4–6 • PREPARATION: 30 MINUTES • COOKING: 20 MINUTES ⇐

1 bunch of basil
½ bunch of flat leaf parsley
8 medium tomatoes
salt
50 ml (2 fl oz) olive oil

4 anchovy fillets
1 garlic clove, cut in two
2 tablespoons dried oregano
65 g (2½ oz) freshly grated Parmesan
75 g (3 oz) homemade breadcrumbs

IN ADVANCE:
Chop the basil and parsley.

1 2
3 4

1	Cut the tomatoes in half, remove the seeds and centres using a spoon, and sprinkle the insides with salt. Invert them on a board and leave to drain.	2	Heat a little oil in a pan and add the anchovies and garlic. Stir until the fillets form a paste. Discard the garlic. Off the heat, mix in the herbs, Parmesan, breadcrumbs and half the oil.
3	Stuff the tomatoes with this mixture using 2 teaspoons then transfer to a baking tray and drizzle with the remaining oil.	4	Cook in a preheated oven at 180°C (350°F), Gas Mark 4 for 20 minutes. Serve as a side dish.

OVEN-BAKED CHERRY TOMATOES

SERVES 4 • PREPARATION: 10 MINUTES • COOKING: 1 HOUR

250 g (8 oz) cherry tomatoes
olive oil
4 pinches of dried oregano (or use snipped
fresh basil leaves)

1 pinch of sugar
salt and freshly ground pepper

1	Cut the tomatoes in half and spread on a baking sheet covered with baking paper. Drizzle with olive oil and season with the oregano, sugar and salt and pepper. Transfer to a preheated oven at 120°C (250°F), Gas Mark ½, and cook for 1 hour.

SERVING IDEAS
❄

Enjoy these tomatoes with mozzarella, in salads, with pasta and rice dishes, with meat, fish…

STORING
❄

☛ Store these tomatoes in a sealed box in the fridge and use within 2–3 days.

OVEN-BAKED VEGETABLE MEDLEY

❖ **SERVES 4–6** • **PREPARATION: 15 MINUTES** • **COOKING: 30 MINUTES** ❖

2 aubergines
1 red pepper
2 carrots
2 courgettes
1 fennel bulb

2 red onions
olive oil
salt and freshly ground pepper
1 tablespoon balsamic vinegar
1 bunch of basil or flat leaf parsley

IN ADVANCE:
Preheat the oven to 200°C (400°F), Gas Mark 6.

1 2
3 4

1	Cut all the vegetables into even-sized chunks.	2	Place them in a baking tray large enough to accommodate them in a single layer. Season with olive oil, salt and pepper.
3	Transfer to the preheated oven and cook for about 30 minutes, turning them 2 or 3 times.	4	Add the balsamic vinegar and snip the basil or parsley on top. Serve warm or at room temperature on little toasts, with couscous or bulgar wheat salad, or as a side dish.

COURGETTE FRITTATA

SERVES 6 • PREPARATION: 20 MINUTES • COOKING: 15 MINUTES

½ bunch of mint + ½ bunch of basil
3 medium courgettes
2 tablespoons olive oil
1 garlic clove

12 eggs
50 g (2 oz) freshly grated Parmesan
salt and freshly ground pepper

IN ADVANCE:
Finely snip the herbs and cut the courgettes into rounds.

1	Heat a little oil in a frying pan, add the garlic and courgettes. Cook, stirring, over a high heat for 5 minutes. Remove the garlic and season.	2	Briskly beat the eggs in a large bowl with a fork. Add the grated Parmesan, the snipped herbs and some salt and pepper.
3	Pour the egg mixture over the courgettes then cook over a medium-high heat, shaking the pan frequently.	4	When the eggs start to set at the edges, bring them into the centre using a wooden spoon. ➤

| 5 | As soon as the base is set, place a large plate over the frying pan and quickly invert it. Add 1 tablespoon of olive oil to the pan then slide the frittata back into the pan to brown on the second side. | **VARIATION**

You can use various vegetables in a frittata: pan-fried artichokes, petits pois, asparagus tips, peppers, and so forth. |

| 6 | The frittata should be golden-brown on the outside and soft inside. | **SERVING IDEAS**
❄
Serve hot, with a salad, or cold as an aperitif, cut into cubes. |

HERB & VEGETABLE PIE

➤ **SERVES 6–8** • **PREPARATION: 50 MINUTES** • **RESTING: 30 MINUTES** • **COOKING: 45 MINUTES** ◄

PASTRY:
250 g (8 oz) plain flour
3 tablespoons olive oil + 1 knob of butter
2 pinches of salt
about 100 ml (3½ fl oz) warm water

FILLING:
600 g (1¼ lb) Swiss chard, washed
500 g (1 lb) frozen spinach, defrosted
olive oil + 50 g (2 oz) butter
75 g (3 oz) smoked bacon or lardons

½ bunch of spring onions with green parts
2 garlic cloves, peeled and chopped
salt, freshly ground pepper and nutmeg
½ bunch flat leaf parsley, chopped
75 g (3 oz) freshly grated Parmesan

1	Mix together the flour and olive oil in a large mixing bowl. Incorporate the butter by hand and add the salt.	2	Stir in enough water (add in stages) so that the mixture comes together to form a non-sticky ball.
3	Turn out and work the dough for a few minutes on a board or work surface.	4	Cover with a clean tea towel and leave to rest for 30 minutes. ➜

5	Meanwhile, prepare the filling. Steam the Swiss chard, allowing 7 minutes for the stalks and 5 minutes for the green leaves. Add the spinach at the end. Drain and allow to cool.	6	Heat 1 tablespoon olive oil in a frying pan, add the smoked bacon (diced if using rashers) and brown on all sides.
7	Add the chopped spring onions (discard the tops of the greens) and garlic. Reduce the heat to very low and leave to cook for 5 minutes.	8	Use your hands to squeeze all the water from the chard and spinach then chop them with a knife (not in a food-processor!).

9 10
11 12

9	Add the chopped greens to the frying pan and allow to dry for a few minutes, stirring. Season with salt, pepper and 2–3 pinches of grated nutmeg.	10	Remove from the heat and allow the mixture to cool then add the chopped parsley and two-thirds of the Parmesan. Taste and adjust the seasoning as necessary.	
11	Flour your work surface and roll out half the pastry very thinly. Use it to line an oiled or non-stick baking tray.	12	Sprinkle the base with the remaining Parmesan then spread the cooked herbs and vegetables on top.	➤

13 Roll out the remaining pastry very finely and cover the filling. Press the edges together to seal well then prick the surface of the pie with the tines of a fork.

		SERVING IDEAS
14	Transfer to a preheated oven at 180°C (350°F), Gas Mark 4 and cook for 30 minutes. Brush the top of the pastry with olive oil and return the pie to the oven to brown.	☞ Allow the pie to cool then cut into portions and serve with salad, or cut into 16 small squares to serve as an aperitif.

MINESTRONE

❧ **SERVES 6** • PREPARATION: 20 MINUTES • COOKING: 1 HOUR • SOAKING: 12 HOURS ☙

600 g (1¼ lb) fresh shelled haricot beans or
200 g (7 oz) dried haricot beans
1 onion + 2 celery stalks
2 carrots
2 potatoes + 2 medium courgettes

2 Swiss chard leaves (green parts only)
100 g (3½ oz) French beans
3 tomatoes, skinned and deseeded
2 tablespoons chopped parsley
olive oil, salt and freshly ground pepper

IN ADVANCE:
If you are using dried beans, soak them in
cold water for 12 hours in advance. Rinse
and drain before adding with the vegetables.

1 2
3 4

1	Chop the onion and peel and cut all the other vegetables into even-sized pieces.	2	Heat 2 tablespoons of olive oil in a large, heavy-based casserole. Add the onion, celery and carrot and cook gently to soften.
3	Add the remaining vegetables, along with the haricot beans. Season with salt and pour in enough water to cover.	4	Leave to simmer over a low heat for 1 hour. At the end of cooking, add the parsley, a drizzle of olive oil and some freshly ground pepper.

BORLOTTI BEAN SOUP

➔ **SERVES 6** • PREPARATION: 15 MINUTES • COOKING: 3 HOURS • SOAKING: 12 HOURS ❖

300 g (10 oz) dried borlotti beans
1 pinch of bicarbonate of soda or a 5-cm
(2-in) piece of kombu
1 onion + 1 garlic clove
1 celery stalk + 1 carrot

100 ml (3½ fl oz) olive oil
25 g (1 oz) bacon or bacon rind in the piece
1 rosemary stalk + 1 bay leaf
salt and freshly ground pepper
2.5 litres (4 pints) water

100 g (3½ oz) tagliatelle, broken in pieces
IN ADVANCE:
Soak the dried beans in cold water for
12 hours in advance with the bicarbonate
or soda or the kombu. Rinse and drain.

1 2
3 4

1	Chop all the vegetables. Heat a little oil in a large stockpot and add in all the vegetables with the bacon, rosemary and bay leaf. Season with salt.	2	Add the borlotti beans and 1 litre (1¾ pints) of water. Bring to the boil then reduce the heat and simmer for 2 hours, adding in extra boiling water as it cooks. Check the seasoning.
3	Blend half the soup in a liquidizer or pass through a vegetable mill.	4	Return the pan to the heat. When it boils, add the tagliatelle and cook until al dente. Serve the soup with a drizzle of olive oil and some pepper.

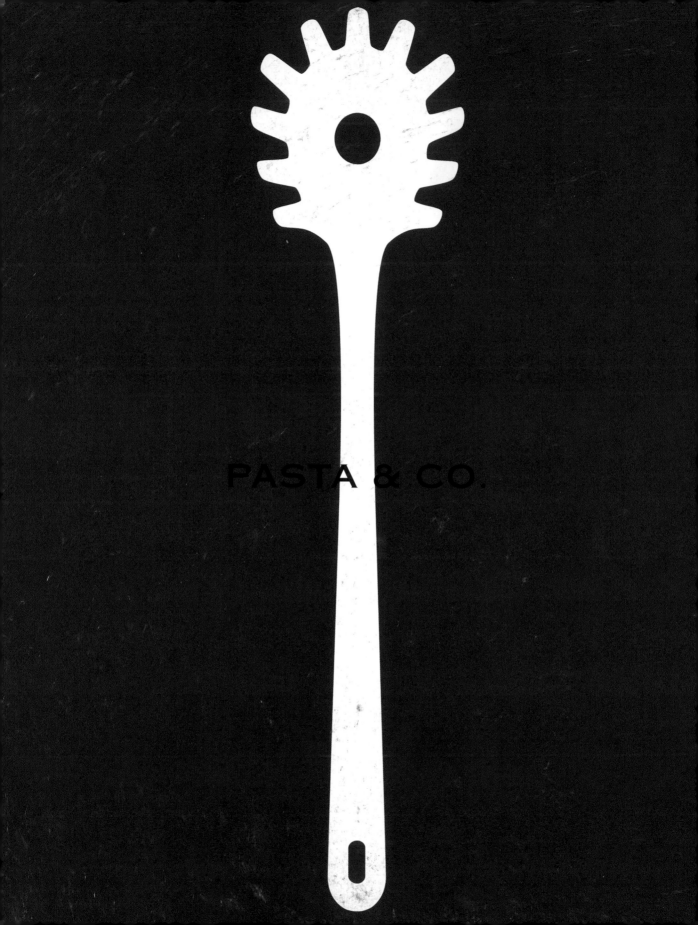

PASTA & CO.

EGG PASTA

Homemade pasta 32
Papardelle with duck sauce 33
Tagliatelle with mushrooms....................... 34
Béchamel sauce 35
Lasagne verde bolognaise......................... 36
Asparagus & pea lasagne 37
Spinach & ricotta crêpes 38
Ravioli stuffed with squash 39

SAUCES

Tomato sauce 40
Anchovy & garlic sauce........................... 41
Chilli & bacon sauce 42

HARD WHEAT PASTA

Carbonara with artichokes........................ 43
Penne with aubergines 44
Bucatini with fresh sardines 45
Linguine with clams 46
Pasta gratin 47
Sicilian-style pasta salad 48
Vegetable-stuffed pasta 49

RISOTTO & GNOCCHI

Classic risotto 50
Saffron risotto 51
Mushroom risotto 52
Squash risotto 53
Leek & cotechino risotto 54
Potato gnocchi 55
Roman-style gnocchi 56

3

HOMEMADE PASTA

❖ **MAKES 800 G (1 LB 10 OZ) PASTA • PREPARATION: 30 MINUTES • RESTING: 1 HOUR** ❖

5 eggs
1–2 tablespoons milk
500 g (1 lb) strong white flour
1 pinch of salt
1 tablespoon olive oil

IN ADVANCE:
Take the eggs and milk from the fridge and bring to room temperature to ensure they mix evenly. Sift the flour with the salt on to a pastry board or work surface.

FOR LASAGNE VERDE:
Add 350 g (12 oz) cooked spinach, squeezed dry and blended, and use 3 not 5 eggs in the recipe.

1	Make a well in the flour and break in the eggs. Mix with a fork.	2	Little by little, incorporate the flour using your fingertips.	
3	Use a spatula to bring in all the flour to make a dough. Work the dough on the board for 10 minutes using the palm of your hand. Add the milk, the olive oil, and a little more flour if necessary.	4	When the dough is smooth and shiny, shape into a ball, cover in cling film and leave to rest for between 30 minutes and up to 2 hours at room temperature.	➤

	TO ROLL OUT THE PASTA
	❄
5	**WITH A PASTA MACHINE:** take about 65 g (2½ oz) of the dough, flatten to a disc shape with the palm of your hand, lightly flour, then put through the machine with the rollers open to the maximum.	**BY HAND:** use a rolling pin, working always from the centre to the edges. Work quickly to prevent the pasta from drying out. The thickness need not be exact but the more even it is, the better the sauce will cling to the pasta.

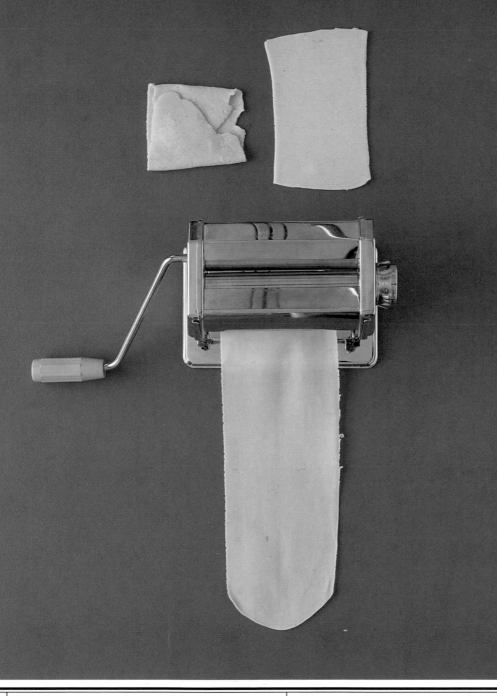

6 Fold the dough in half or in three before putting it through the pasta machine to produce a thin sheet. Feed it through several times, each time tightening the rollers, until you have a thin, even sheet.

TIP

Roll only a little dough at a time, keeping the remainder in a plastic bag so that it doesn't dry out.

➢

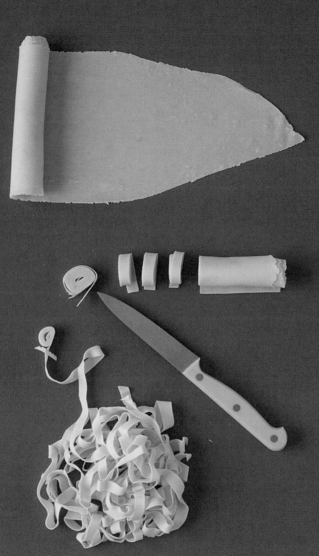

TO MAKE TAGLIATELLE
❋

| 7 | Leave the sheets of pasta to dry out slightly (otherwise they will stick), then roll them up and cut them into ribbons 1 cm (½ in) wide. | ☛ Unroll the ribbons and arrange in a nest on a tray made of cardboard with holes in it (so that the air can circulate. Cover and keep them dry. Cook within 2 days. |

8

A 65-g (2½-oz) block of dough makes lasagne sheets 10–12 cm (4–5 in) wide and 40 cm (16 in) long to trim according to your dish size. To make papardelle and tagliolini, follow the method for making tagliatelle but cut them into ribbons 2 cm (under 1 in) and ½ cm (¼ in) wide respectively. Maltagliati are roughly cut pieces made from the trimmings.

TIP
☛ For a firmer pasta, use one-third semolina and two-thirds wheat flour, instead of all flour.

COOKING PASTA
Allow 1 litre (1¾ pints) water and ½ teaspoon salt for every 75 g (3 oz) portion of pasta.

PAPARDELLE WITH DUCK SAUCE

❧ SERVES 6–8 • PREPARATION: 40 MINUTES • COOKING: 1 HOUR ❧

DUCK SAUCE:
100 g (3½ oz) carrots
100 g (3½ oz) onions
100 g (3½ oz) celery stalks
2 garlic cloves
1 duck, quartered

2 rosemary stalks
1 tablespoon olive oil
100 ml (3½ fl oz) dry white wine
500 ml (17 fl oz) vegetable stock
400 g (14 oz) tinned tomatoes
salt and freshly ground pepper

700 g (1½ lb) fresh papardelle (see recipe 32)
65 g (2½ oz) butter
100 g (3½ oz) Parmesan

IN ADVANCE:
Finely chop the vegetables.

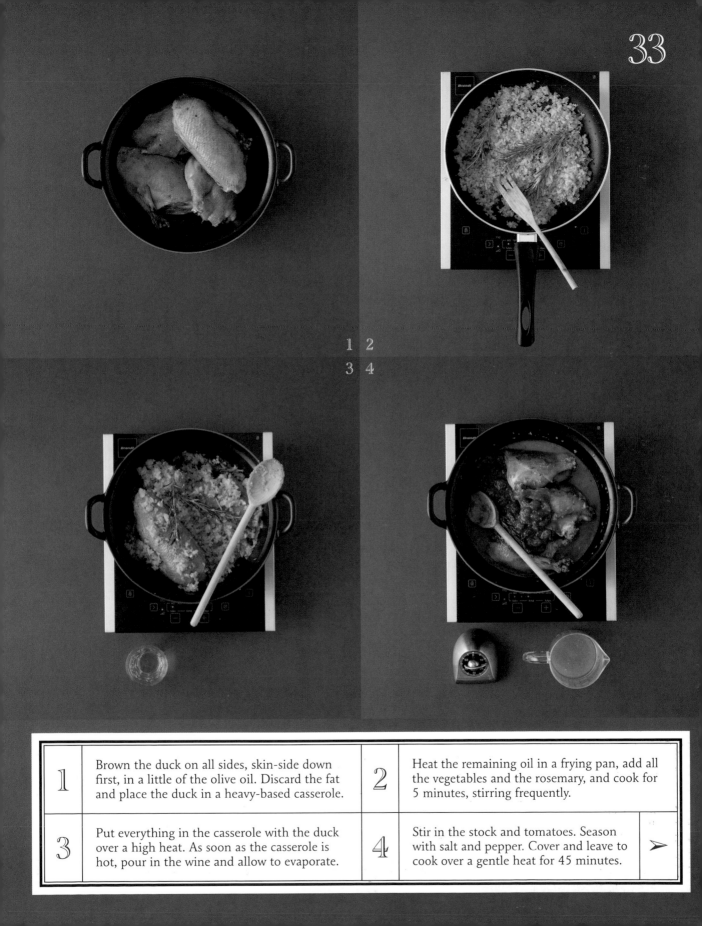

1	Brown the duck on all sides, skin-side down first, in a little of the olive oil. Discard the fat and place the duck in a heavy-based casserole.	2	Heat the remaining oil in a frying pan, add all the vegetables and the rosemary, and cook for 5 minutes, stirring frequently.
3	Put everything in the casserole with the duck over a high heat. As soon as the casserole is hot, pour in the wine and allow to evaporate.	4	Stir in the stock and tomatoes. Season with salt and pepper. Cover and leave to cook over a gentle heat for 45 minutes. ➤

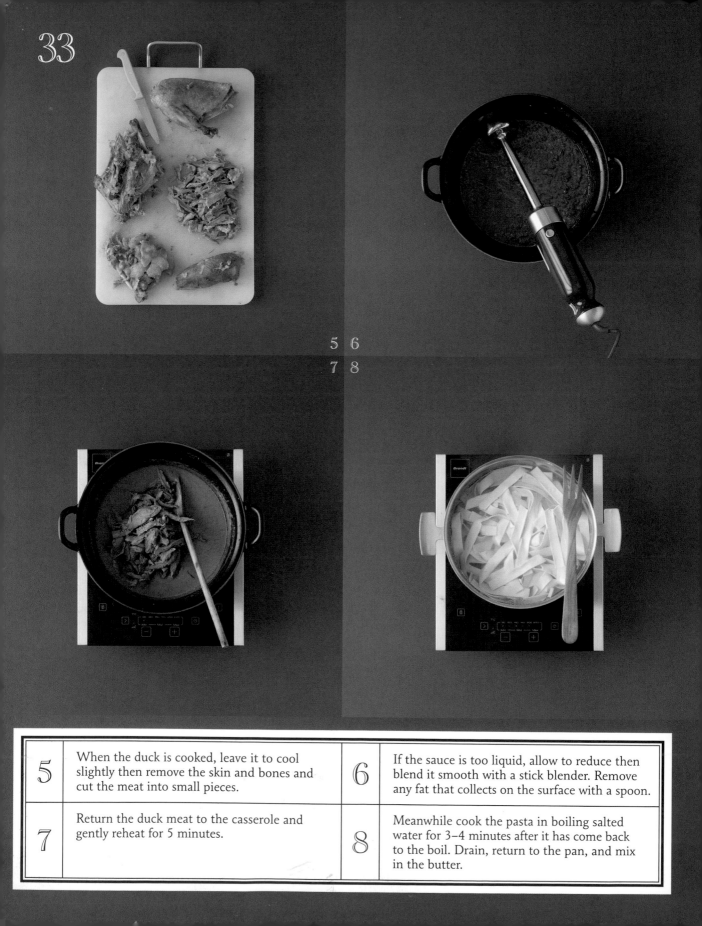

5 6
7 8

5	When the duck is cooked, leave it to cool slightly then remove the skin and bones and cut the meat into small pieces.	6	If the sauce is too liquid, allow to reduce then blend it smooth with a stick blender. Remove any fat that collects on the surface with a spoon.
7	Return the duck meat to the casserole and gently reheat for 5 minutes.	8	Meanwhile cook the pasta in boiling salted water for 3–4 minutes after it has come back to the boil. Drain, return to the pan, and mix in the butter.

9	Top the pasta with the duck sauce and serve with the grated Parmesan.

VARIATION
※

This sauce can also be used to make a lasagne, layered with a little Béchamel Sauce (see recipe 35).

TIP
※

☞ If possible, prepare the duck sauce the day before. When cooled, the fat will solidify, making it easier to remove from the surface.

TAGLIATELLE WITH MUSHROOMS

⤜ SERVES 4 • PREPARATION: 45 MINUTES • COOKING: 30 MINUTES ⤛

MUSHROOM SAUCE:
600 g (1¼ lb) mixed wild mushrooms
(ceps, girolles, oyster, and so forth)
2 tablespoons olive oil
40 g (1½ oz) butter + 2 extra knobs

salt and freshly ground pepper
2 garlic cloves
½ bunch flat leaf parsley
500 g (1 lb) fresh tagliatelle (see recipe 32)
25 g (1 oz) freshly grated Parmesan

IN ADVANCE:
Clean the mushrooms, scraping them with a
knife to remove the soil. Plunge them twice
into water, remove immediately and wipe dry.

1	Cut the biggest mushrooms into halves or thirds then spread them out to dry on a clean tea towel.	2	Heat the oil with the 2 knobs of butter and the garlic. Add the mushrooms and cook over a high heat to release their water. Do not stir.
3	Season with salt and pepper, add a little chopped parsley and leave to cook for a further 3 minutes over a gentle heat (discard the garlic). Keep warm.	4	Cook the tagliatelle until al dente. Put a little of the cooking water into a frying pan, melt the butter, then stir in the drained tagliatelle, the mushrooms and the Parmesan.

BÉCHAMEL SAUCE

➤ **ENOUGH TO MAKE 1 LASAGNE** • PREPARATION: 10 MINUTES • COOKING: 15 MINUTES ◄

75 g (3 oz) butter
75 g (3 oz) plain flour
1 litre (1¾ pints) milk

4 pinches freshly grated nutmeg
salt

1	Melt the butter in a saucepan over a gentle heat.	2	Sprinkle the flour over the top, stirring with a whisk.	3	When the mixture starts to take on colour, gradually add the milk.
4	Stir constantly to prevent any lumps forming.	5	Leave to cook gently for 10 minutes. Add the nutmeg and salt.	6	Allow to cool; if the sauce is too thick, stir in a little more milk.

LASAGNE VERDE BOLOGNAISE

❧ SERVES 6 • PREPARATION: 1 HOUR 30 MINUTES • COOKING: 1 HOUR 30 MINUTES – 2 HOURS ❧

25 g (1 oz) dried ceps (wild mushrooms)
100 g (3½ oz) carrots
100 g (3½ oz) onions
100 g (3½ oz) celery stalks
3 tablespoons olive oil
350 g (12 oz) stewing beef, cubed small

350 g (12 oz) shoulder of veal, cubed small
150 ml (¼ pint) red wine
salt and pepper
250 ml (8 fl oz) vegetable stock
fresh herbs, tied as a bouquet garni
2 cloves

400 g (14 oz) tinned tomatoes
8–12 spinach lasagne sheets (see recipe 32)
25 g (1 oz) butter
Béchamel Sauce (see recipe 35)
150 g (5 oz) Parmesan

1	Soak the dried mushrooms for 30 minutes in 250 ml (8 fl oz) warm water. Strain the soaking water and reserve.	2	Finely chop all the vegetables.
3	Heat the oil in a heavy-based casserole, add the meat and all the chopped vegetables and cook over a high heat, stirring, for 20–30 minutes.	4	When the mixture starts to catch on the base of the casserole, pour in the wine. Allow the liquid to evaporate.

5 6
7 8

5	Season with salt, add the mushrooms, soaking water, stock, herbs and cloves. Simmer for 1 hour, adding the tomatoes halfway through.	6	To cook the lasagne, lower the sheets, 3 or 4 at a time, into a large pan of boiling salted water with a little olive oil. Cook for 2–3 minutes.
7	Immediately put the sheets in a bowl of cold water to stop the cooking, drain, then spread them out on a clean tea towel without any overlapping.	8	Butter a gratin dish, pour a little Béchamel into the base, then build up alternate layers of lasagne, Béchamel and bolognaise sauce, sprinkling Parmesan on each layer.

9   Continue to build up layers, ending with one of Béchamel mixed with 4 tablespoons of the bolognaise sauce. Sprinkle with Parmesan, and dot with little bits of butter. Transfer to the oven preheated to 180°C (350°F), Gas Mark 4 for 30 minutes. Remove from the oven and allow to rest for 5 minutes before cutting into portions. Buon appetito!

TIP

☞ You can of course make this dish with plain lasagne. It's best to precook the sheets in advance.

VARIATION

Serve tagliatelle with this bolognaise sauce, as they do in Emilia Romagna.

ASPARAGUS & PEA LASAGNE

⇢ SERVES 6 • PREPARATION: 40 MINUTES • COOKING: 50 MINUTES ⇠

1 kg (2 lb) fresh peas in the pod (or 250 g/
8 oz shelled peas)
1 bunch of green asparagus spears
1 bunch of spring or early crop onions
2–3 tablespoons olive oil

3–4 knobs of butter
salt
8–12 lasagne sheets (see recipe 32)
Béchamel Sauce (see recipe 35)
500 g (1 lb) burrata or ricotta

100 g (3½ oz) Parmesan
grated nutmeg
IN ADVANCE:
Shell the peas.

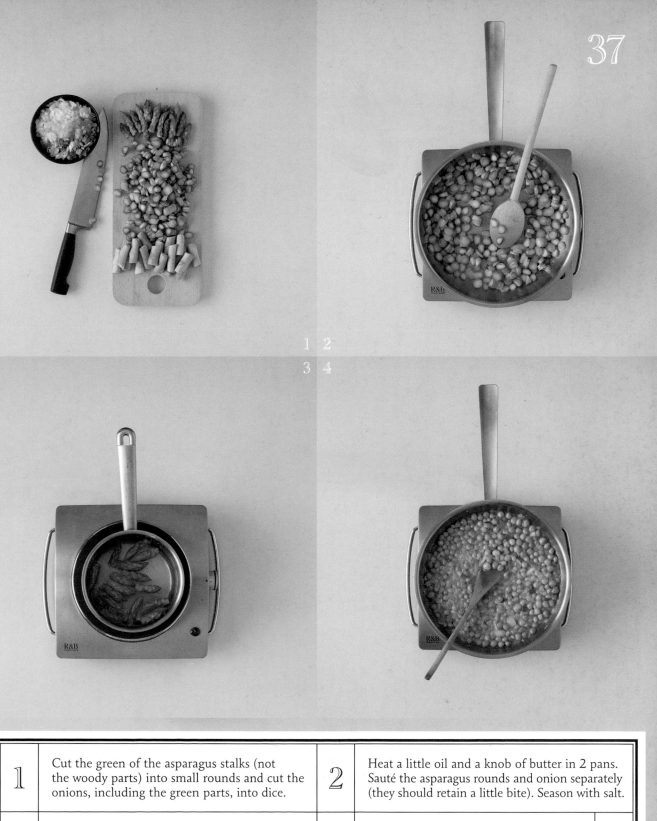

1	Cut the green of the asparagus stalks (not the woody parts) into small rounds and cut the onions, including the green parts, into dice.	2	Heat a little oil and a knob of butter in 2 pans. Sauté the asparagus rounds and onion separately (they should retain a little bite). Season with salt.
3	Bring a small pan of salted water to the boil, drop in the asparagus tips and boil for 2–3 minutes, drain, then set aside.	4	Cook the shelled peas over a gentle heat in a little salted water until tender. ➤

5	To cook the lasagne, lower the sheets, 3 or 4 at a time, into a large pan of boiling salted water with a little olive oil. Cook for 2–3 minutes.	6	Immediately put the sheets in a bowl of cold water to stop the cooking, drain, then spread them out on a clean tea towel without any overlapping.
7	Butter a gratin dish and build up alternate layers of lasagne, Béchamel, vegetables and crumbled cheese. Sprinkle with Parmesan.	8	Continue to build up a further two sets of layers, ending with lasagne then crumbled cheese and a sprinkling of Parmesan.

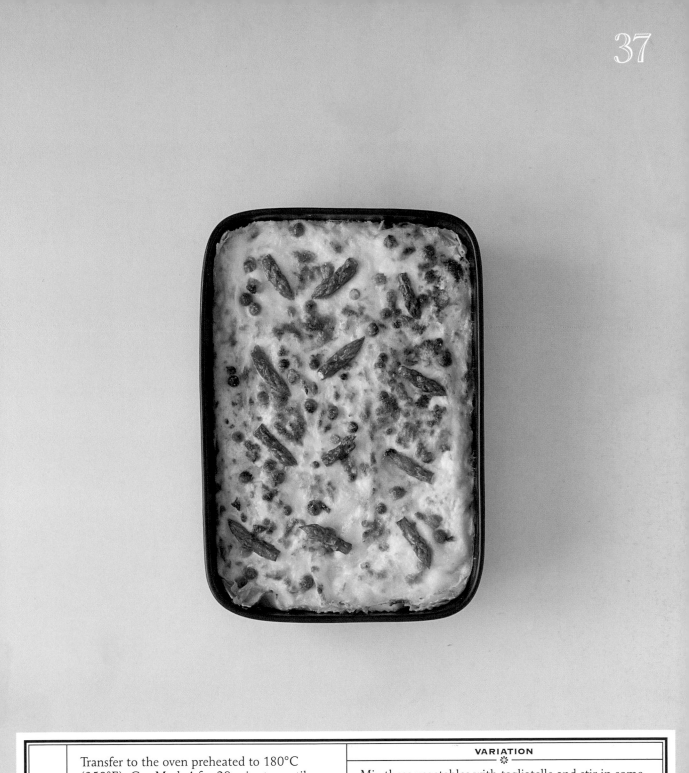

9   Transfer to the oven preheated to 180°C
(350°F), Gas Mark 4 for 20 minutes until
browned and bubbling. Just before serving,
melt a knob of butter in a pan. Toss the
reserved asparagus tips in the butter and
use to garnish the lasagne.

VARIATION
❊

Mix these vegetables with tagliatelle and stir in some
melted butter with a little of the pasta cooking water.

TIP
❊

☛ If you don't have time to make your own pasta,
buy good-quality dried lasagne sheets made with eggs
which you will find in Italian delicatessens.

SPINACH & RICOTTA CRÊPES

→ **SERVES 6** • **PREPARATION: 1 HOUR** • **RESTING: 1 HOUR** • **COOKING: 1 HOUR** ←

CRÊPE BATTER:
125 g (4 oz) flour
3 eggs
salt
20 g (¾ oz) melted butter
250 ml (8 fl oz) milk

FILLING:
600 g (1¼ lb) fresh or 300 g (10 oz) frozen spinach
1 tablespoon olive oil + 50 g (2 oz) butter
1 garlic clove, cut in half
salt and freshly ground pepper

few pinches of grated nutmeg
250 g (8 oz) ricotta + 125 g (4 oz) mascarpone
2 tablespoons breadcrumbs
75 g (3 oz) freshly grated Parmesan
IN ADVANCE:
Steam the spinach, drain and squeeze dry.

1	First make the batter. Put the flour in a mixing bowl and make a well in the centre. Add the eggs, salt and melted butter. Whisk together.	2	Stir in the milk, whisking constantly to avoid any lumps. Cover the bowl with cling film and leave to rest for 1 hour.
3	Heat a frying pan with the oil, half the butter and the garlic. Dry the spinach over a medium heat. Season with salt, pepper and nutmeg.	4	Put in a bowl to cool. Add the ricotta, mascarpone, breadcrumbs and 50 g (2 oz) of Parmesan. Check the seasoning.

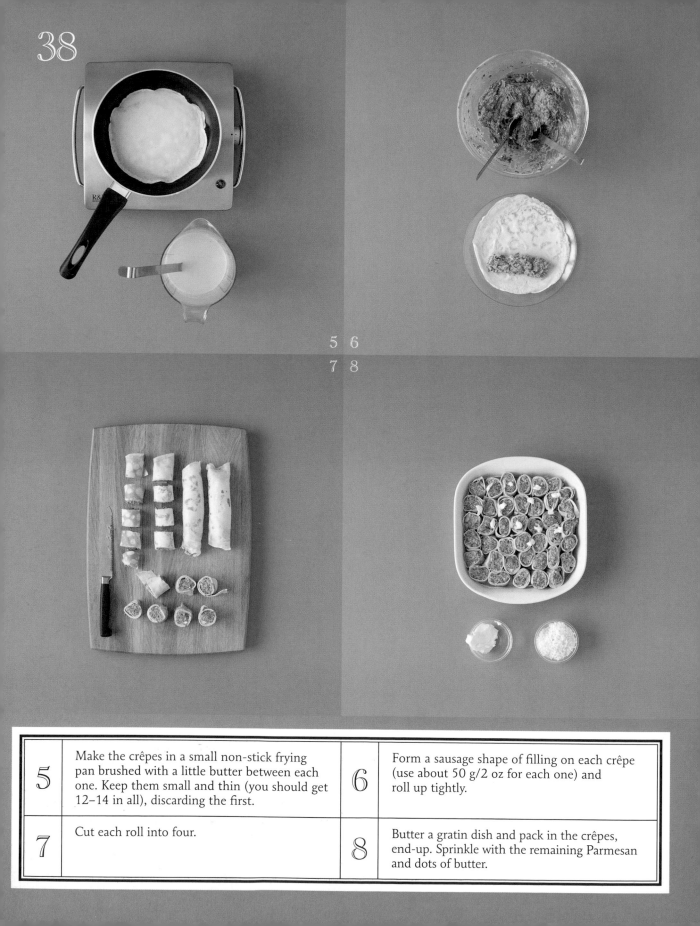

5 6
7 8

5	Make the crêpes in a small non-stick frying pan brushed with a little butter between each one. Keep them small and thin (you should get 12–14 in all), discarding the first.	6	Form a sausage shape of filling on each crêpe (use about 50 g/2 oz for each one) and roll up tightly.
7	Cut each roll into four.	8	Butter a gratin dish and pack in the crêpes, end-up. Sprinkle with the remaining Parmesan and dots of butter.

| 9 | Brown in a preheated oven at 200°C (400°F), Gas Mark 6. It's ready! | **VARIATION**
❋
These crêpes can be used to replace lasagne sheets. You can stuff them with Bolognaise Sauce (see recipe 36), with a little Béchamel Sauce or with such vegetables as asparagus or peas (see recipe 37). |

RAVIOLI STUFFED WITH SQUASH

➤ **SERVES 10** • PREPARATION: 1 HOUR • COOKING: 50 MINUTES ◆

FILLING:
75 g (3 oz) apple condiment or 60 g (2½ oz)
Mostarda di Cremona
50 g (2 oz) amaretti di Saronno
1 kg (2 lb) squash (acorn, buttercup etc)

3 pinches grated nutmeg
2 pinches cinnamon
100 g (3½ oz) freshly grated Parmesan
800 g (1 lb 10 oz) Homemade Pasta
(see recipe 32)

salt and white pepper
knob of butter per person + 12 sage leaves
IN ADVANCE:
Blend the mostarda to a smooth purée.
Crush the amaretti.

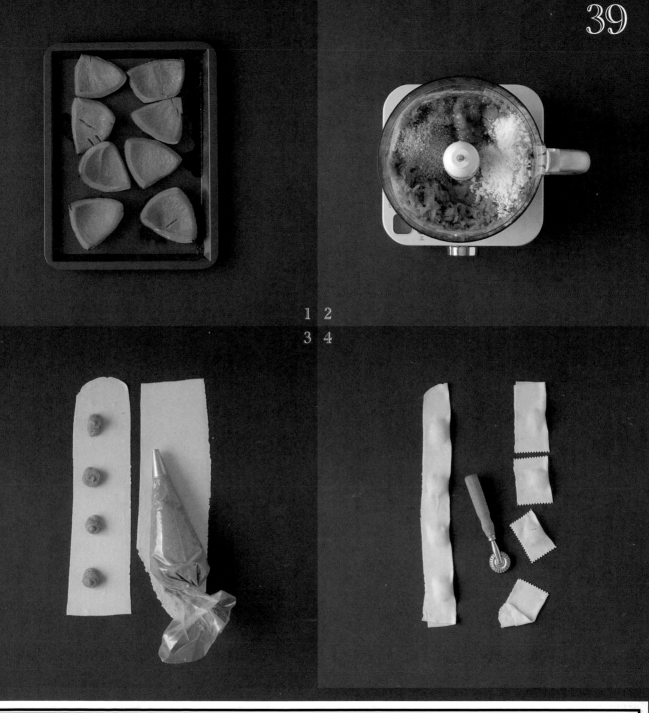

1	Cut up the squash and remove the seeds and fibres. Bake in a preheated oven at 180°C (350°F), Gas Mark 4 for 40 minutes until tender.	2	Blend the cooked squash, then add the spices, amaretti, mostarda, 40 g (1½ oz) of the Parmesan, salt and pepper.
3	Roll out the pasta into very thin sheets. Use a piping bag (or a teaspoon), to make regularly spaced (5 cm/2 in apart) little heaps of stuffing in the middle of the pasta.	4	Fold over the pasta to enclose the filling. Press around the filling with your fingers to seal each one and remove air pockets. Use a ravioli cutter to make parcels. ➢

| 5 | Cook the ravioli, 3 or 4 portions at a time, in a large pan of lightly salted simmering water for about 3 minutes. Remove, drain and place in serving bowls with a helping of sage butter (see opposite) on each portion. | **SAGE BUTTER**
❈

Melt a knob of butter per person over a gentle heat with the sage leaves and a little water. |

6	Serve hot, with freshly grated Parmesan.	**TIP** ❀ ☛ If the pasta has dried a little, brush the edges with a wash of egg white and a little water.
PREPARATION IN ADVANCE ❀		**VARIATIONS** ❀
☛ You can make your ravioli the day before and keep them, covered, on a tray in the fridge, between two clean tea towels, or freeze them spread out flat.		Use the spinach and ricotta filling (recipe 38) or grated cheese (150 g/5 oz ricotta and 200 g/7 oz mild Pecorino and 125 g/4 oz Parmesan and 1 egg).

TOMATO SAUCE

SERVES 4–6 • PREPARATION: 15 MINUTES • COOKING: 30 MINUTES

1 onion, 1 carrot, 1 celery stalk
1 kg (2 lb) ripe plum tomatoes or 800 g
(1 lb 10 oz) tinned chopped tomatoes

2 tablespoons olive oil
handful of basil
salt

ALTERNATIVE:
Replace the vegetables with 1 large onion
or 2 garlic cloves, softened in a frying pan.

1 2
3 4

1	Finely chop the onion, carrot and celery. If you are using fresh tomatoes, cut into quarters, remove the seeds and cut the flesh into pieces.	2	Heat the olive oil in a pan, add the vegetables and cook for 10 minutes until softened. Add the tomatoes, half the basil and a little salt.
3	Cook over a high heat for 2 minutes then for 15 minutes over a medium heat, stirring regularly. Pass through a vegetable mill.	4	Add the remaining basil. The sauce will keep in the fridge for 2–3 days in a jar covered with a layer of olive oil.

ANCHOVY & GARLIC SAUCE

❧ **FOR 250 G (8 OZ) OF PASTA** • PREPARATION: 10 MINUTES • COOKING: 20 MINUTES ❧

Heat 2 tablespoons of olive oil in a frying pan and soften 3 anchovy fillets. Add 1 garlic clove and 1 tablespoon of rinsed chopped capers. Stir for 1 minute then add the chopped tomatoes, 2 pinches of chilli powder and 50 g (2 oz) of pitted black olives, cut into rounds. Cook for 2 minutes over a high heat then for 8–10 minutes over a medium heat, stirring often. At the end, add salt and 2 tablespoons chopped flat leaf parsley. (Note: there is no cheese in this version; it doesn't go well with fish!)

CHILLI & BACON SAUCE

❖ **FOR 250 G (8 OZ) OF PASTA** • PREPARATION: 10 MINUTES • COOKING: 20 MINUTES ❖

Heat 2 tablespoons of olive oil in a frying pan and soften 1 chopped onion and 75 g (3 oz) of pancetta cut into small dice. Add the chopped tomatoes and 2 pinches of chilli powder. Cook over a high heat for 2 minutes then for a further 8–10 minutes over a medium heat, stirring often. At the end, add salt to taste and generous amounts of ground pepper and sprinkle with freshly grated Pecorino or Parmesan.

CARBONARA WITH ARTICHOKES

❧ **SERVES 4** • PREPARATION: 30 MINUTES • COOKING: 20 MINUTES ❧

50 ml (2 fl oz) olive oil
4 small purple artichokes (poivrades)
1 garlic clove
1 tablespoon chopped flat leaf parsley
½ glass white wine or vegetable stock

salt and freshly ground pepper
350 g (12 oz) spaghettoni (large spaghetti)
125 g (4 oz) fatty pancetta or lardons
1 whole egg + 3 egg yolks
75 g (3 oz) freshly grated Parmesan

IN ADVANCE:
Prepare the artichokes and cut them into
fine slices (see recipe 21). Cut the pancetta
into dice.

1 2
3 4

1	Heat 2 tablespoons of the oil and cook the artichokes with the garlic and parsley. Add the wine and let it evaporate. Season with salt and pepper. The artichokes should retain some bite.	2	Cook the pasta in a large pan of boiling salted water until al dente.	
3	Heat a little oil in a second frying pan and brown the pancetta on all sides.	4	Mix the eggs with the Parmesan, a little more oil and salt and pepper. Moisten with a little of the pasta cooking water.	➤

5   Put the drained pasta in a large bowl with
2 or 3 tablespoons olive oil and the pancetta.
Add in the egg mixture and the artichokes.
Combine thoroughly.

| 6 | Grind plenty of pepper on top and serve immediately. | **TRADITIONAL CARBONARA**
❋
☛ In Italy spaghetti alla carbonara was traditionally prepared with salted pork cheek instead of pancetta, and without artichokes or creamy sauce! |

PENNE WITH AUBERGINES

➤ SERVES 4 • PREPARATION: 20 MINUTES • COOKING: 20 MINUTES ➤

2 aubergines
50 ml (2 fl oz) olive oil
1 garlic clove
400 g (14 fl oz) Tomato Sauce (see recipe 40)
handful of basil

350 g (12 oz) penne
100 g (3½ oz) fresh or salted ricotta, crumbled
50 g (2 oz) Pecorino or Parmesan, grated
freshly ground pepper

IN ADVANCE:
Cut the aubergines into cubes.

1	Heat a frying pan with 2 tablespoons olive oil and the garlic then add some of the aubergines (work in batches, not to overcrowd the pan).	2	Cook the aubergines over a gentle heat, stirring often, until they are soft and coloured. Return all the cooked aubergines to the pan at the end.
3	Add the tomato sauce and half the basil. Allow to bubble gently for a few minutes.	4	Cook the pasta until al dente, drain then mix with the sauce. Serve garnished with the ricotta, Pecorino, pepper and the remaining basil.

BUCATINI WITH FRESH SARDINES

⇛ SERVES 4 • PREPARATION: 30 MINUTES • COOKING: 50 MINUTES ⇚

8–10 fresh whole sardines + 4 to garnish
25 g (1 oz) small raisins
1 fennel bulb + 1 teaspoon fennel seeds
olive oil
1 large onion, finely chopped

20 g (¾ oz) pine nuts
2 pinches powdered saffron or a few threads
2 anchovy fillets, rinsed and chopped
salt and freshly ground pepper
500 g (1 lb) bucatini (thick spaghetti)

IN ADVANCE:
Clean the sardines and remove the heads
and backbones to give 2 fillets per fish (see
recipe 61). Soak the raisins for 15 minutes
in warm water.

1 2
3 4

1	Bring 4 litres (7 pints) of water to the boil. Add the fennel, cut in half, and the seeds. Cook for 15 minutes then drain, reserving the water.	2	Heat 1 tablespoon of olive oil. Add the onion, soften for 2 minutes then add 1 glass of the fennel cooking water. Allow to reduce by half.	
3	Add 4 more tablespoons of oil and the raisins, pine nuts, saffron and fennel. Allow to simmer for 5 minutes.	4	Add the sardines (reserving 4 as garnish) and the anchovies. Lightly season with salt and pepper and cook for a further 5 minutes, stirring, over a gentle heat.	➤

| 5 | Heat a little olive oil in a frying pan and fry the remaining 4 sardines on both sides until they start to colour. (You can dust them first with a little flour if you wish.) Remove the sardines and keep warm. | **COOKING THE PASTA**
❋
Bring the reserved fennel cooking water to the boil in a large pan (topped up with fresh water if necessary), add some salt and cook the pasta until al dente. Drain thoroughly. |

| 6 | Sauté the pasta in the oil in which you fried the 4 sardines then add the sauce and the rest of the sardines. Garnish the dish with the reserved fried sardines and serve. | **GRATIN VERSION**
❊
Prepare the sauce using all the sardines. Cook then drain the pasta and dress with oil. In a large oiled gratin dish, alternate layers of pasta and sauce, ending with a layer of sauce. Top with breadcrumbs and pine nuts then put in the oven to brown before serving. |

LINGUINE WITH CLAMS

❧ SERVES 2 • PREPARATION: 40 MINUTES • COOKING: 30 MINUTES ❧

500 g (1 lb) clams, in the shell
1–2 tablespoons olive oil
2 garlic cloves
½ bunch of flat leaf parsley, chopped

few pinches mild dried chilli
100 ml (3½ fl oz) dry white wine
salt and freshly ground pepper
200 g (7 oz) linguine or spaghetti

IN ADVANCE:
Carefully wash the clams in plenty of cold running water. Discard any with shells that remain open.

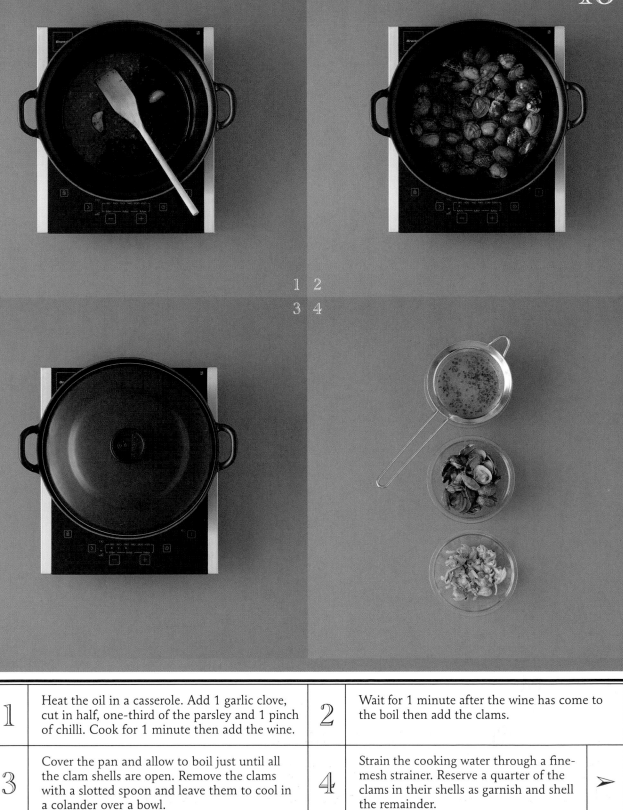

1	Heat the oil in a casserole. Add 1 garlic clove, cut in half, one-third of the parsley and 1 pinch of chilli. Cook for 1 minute then add the wine.	2	Wait for 1 minute after the wine has come to the boil then add the clams.
3	Cover the pan and allow to boil just until all the clam shells are open. Remove the clams with a slotted spoon and leave them to cool in a colander over a bowl.	4	Strain the cooking water through a fine-mesh strainer. Reserve a quarter of the clams in their shells as garnish and shell the remainder.

5 6
7 8

5	Heat 1 tablespoon of oil and add the second garlic clove (then remove and discard it), the remaining chilli, 2 pinches of parsley and the clam cooking water. Allow to reduce then salt.	6	Meanwhile bring a large pan of salted water to the boil and cook the linguine until al dente.
7	Just before the pasta is cooked, add the shelled clams to their cooking juices.	8	Drain the linguine and toss in the pan with the clams and 2 tablespoons of olive oil.

		VARIATION
9	Serve hot, with a good grinding of pepper, the remaining chopped parsley and the reserved clams in their shells as garnish.	All or a portion of the clams may be replaced by mussels (preparation and cooking steps are identical).

PASTA GRATIN

❧ **SERVES 6** • PREPARATION: 30 MINUTES • COOKING: 20 MINUTES ❧

500 g (1 lb) paccheri (large tube pasta)
250 g (8 oz) mozzarella
150 g smoked Provola
100 g (3½ oz) Parmesan
600 g (1¼ lb) Tomato Sauce (see recipe 40)

handful of basil
20 g (¾ oz) butter
4–6 tablespoons breadcrumbs
250 g (8 oz) ricotta
salt and freshly ground pepper

IN ADVANCE:
Bring a large pan of salted water to the boil then cook the pasta until al dente. Drain.

1 2
3 4

1	Cut the mozzarella and the Provola into small pieces and grate the Parmesan.	2	Mix the cooked pasta with the tomato sauce, half the Parmesan and some basil leaves.
3	Butter a gratin dish, sprinkle the base with breadcrumbs, pour in half the pasta mixture and cover with half the mozzarella, Provola and crumbled ricotta. Top with the remaining basil then repeat the pasta and cheese layers.	4	Sprinkle with breadcrumbs and the remaining Parmesan and dot with butter. Season with salt and pepper. Put in a preheated oven at 180°C (350°F), Gas Mark 4 for about 20 minutes until the top is crisp and golden-brown.

SICILIAN-STYLE PASTA SALAD

❧ **SERVES 6** • PREPARATION: 10 MINUTES • COOKING: 8 MINUTES ❧

250 g (8 oz) cherry tomatoes
salt and freshly ground pepper
50 g (2 oz) mi-cuit tomatoes in olive oil
50 g (2 oz) pitted black taggiasca olives

25 g (1 oz) salted capers, rinsed
extra virgin olive oil
2 tablespoons dried oregano
350 g (12 oz) penne or pennoni

200 g (7 oz) loin of tuna in olive oil (or
white tuna preserved in olive oil)

1	Cut the cherry tomatoes in half and sprinkle with salt. Roughly chop the mi-cuit tomatoes, the olives and the capers.	2	Mix all these ingredients with 4 tablespoons of the olive oil, the oregano, salt and pepper.
3	Cook the pasta until al dente, then drain and rinse immediately under cold running water to stop the cooking. Spread out on a baking tray and drizzle with oil to stop them sticking.	4	Combine the pasta with the vegetables. Add the tuna, separated into large chunks, and more olive oil, if necessary. Taste and adjust the seasoning.

PASTA STUFFED WITH VEGETABLES

⇝ SERVES 4–6 • PREPARATION: 30 MINUTES • COOKING: 30 MINUTES ⇜

2 aubergines
2 medium courgettes
2 peppers of different colours

2 garlic cloves
salt
50–60 ml (2–2½ fl oz) olive oil

500 g (1 lb) conchiglioni (or other large pasta)
6 tablespoons classic pesto (see recipe 01)

1 2
3 4

1	Wash the vegetables and cut them all into small dice.	2	Cook them separately in 1 tablespoon of oil with 1 garlic clove (remove at the end), and salt. The courgettes and peppers should retain a little bite; the aubergines should be soft.	
3	Place all the cooked vegetables in the same frying pan and allow them to gently cook for a few minutes.	4	Cook the pasta until al dente, drain and immediately rinse under cold running water. Spread on a sheet and oil them.	➤

5 Put a small spoonful of the pesto in each pasta shell then fill with 1 tablespoon of vegetables.

VARIATION
※

Stuff the pasta with 1 tablespoon of Caponata (see recipe 23) or with 2 parts ricotta mixed with 1 part Classic Pesto (see recipe 01) or Pistachio Pesto (see recipe 03). You can also mix the pasta with the vegetables and pesto as a salad.

6	It's ready!	**SERVING** ❉ This dish is best served at room temperature, either as something to nibble with drinks or as a summer starter.

GARNISH
❉

You can garnish the shells with a basil leaf, a few grilled pine nuts, or shavings of Parmesan.

CLASSIC RISOTTO

❧ **SERVES 4 • PREPARATION: 10 MINUTES • COOKING: 25 MINUTES** ❧

1.2 litres (2 pints) meat or vegetable stock
1 onion
1 tablespoon olive oil + 10 g (1½ oz) butter
300 g (10 oz) risotto rice (carnaroli, arborio or vialone nano)

salt
50 ml (2 fl oz) dry white wine (or extra stock)
40 g (1½ oz) freshly grated Parmesan, and a few shaving to garnish
40 g (1½ oz) cold butter, cubed

IN ADVANCE:
Heat the stock and keep it at a gentle simmer. Finely chop the onion.

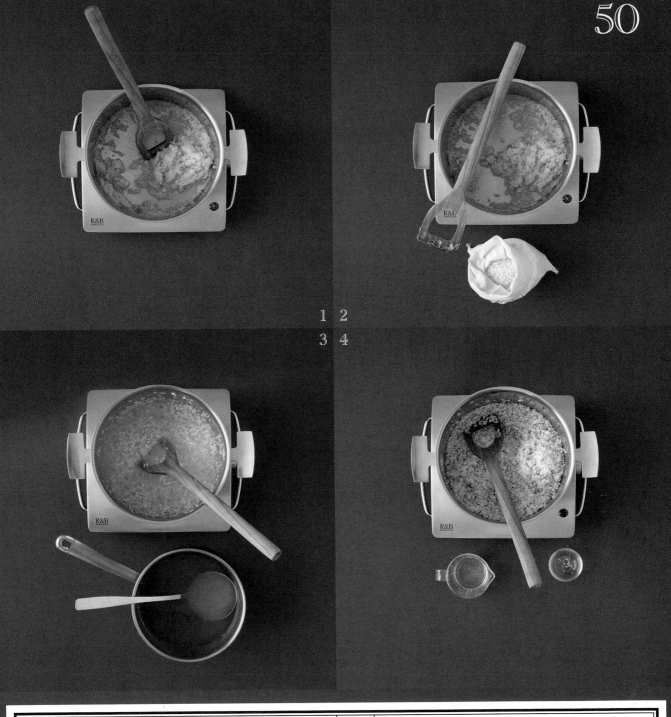

1 2
3 4

1	Heat the oil and 10 g (½ oz) of the butter in a heavy-based saucepan. Add the onion and cook gently for 5 minutes to soften.	2	Turn up the heat and add the rice (no need to wash it). Stir for 2 minutes until the grains are translucent but not coloured. Season with salt, add the wine and stir until it is all absorbed.	
3	Pour in 1 ladleful of hot stock and cook over a medium heat for 15 minutes. Keep adding a ladle of stock as soon as the liquid is absorbed.	4	Five minutes before the end of cooking, taste and adjust the seasoning if necessary.	➤

5	Switch off the heat and add the cold butter and the Parmesan. Stir in rapidly then cover the pan and leave to rest for 2 minutes before serving.

HOMEMADE STOCK

Bring to the boil 2 litres (3½ pints) water with 2 onions, 2 carrots, 2 celery stalks and 2 leeks. Add salt and cook for 40 minutes then strain off the liquid. When you're pressed for time, use good-quality organic stock cubes. For meat stock, add to the vegetable base 500 g (1 lb) side of beef, a chicken or chicken thighs, and cook for 2 hours.

6	It's ready! Serve immediately because the risotto will continue to cook in its own heat.

VARIATION
❋

If any risotto is left over, shape into little cakes, dip into beaten egg then breadcrumbs and brown in a frying pan.

WHICH VARIETY OF RISOTTO RICE?
❋

✧ Carnaroli is the easiest to cook without losing its shape.

✧ Arborio is the most widely available variety.

✧ Vialone nano is the rice of the Veneto, the region around Venice. It is ideal for very liquid risottos.

SAFFRON RISOTTO

➤ SERVES 4 • PREPARATION: 15 MINUTES • COOKING: 20 MINUTES ◄

Assemble the ingredients for a Classic Risotto (see recipe 50). Pour a ladleful of hot stock in a bowl, add 1 pinch of saffron threads and leave to infuse.

Cook one beef marrow bone for 3 minutes in the stock then remove the bone, extract the marrow and cut into pieces. Follow the steps for Classic Risotto, adding the marrow

pieces at the beginning with the onion and soften everything for 10 minutes. Add the saffron and its stock about three-quarters of the way into the cooking period.

MUSHROOM RISOTTO

❧ **SERVES 4** • **PREPARATION: 30 MINUTES** • **COOKING: 30 MINUTES** ❧

Clean 600 g (1¼ lb) of fresh mushrooms. Heat 1 tablespoon of olive oil, 1 knob of butter and 1 whole garlic clove in a frying pan. Add the mushrooms and cook without stirring until they release all their liquid. Season with salt and pepper, lower the heat and cook for a further 2–3 minutes. Discard the garlic, add ½ teaspoon chopped parsley and keep warm. Follow the steps for Classic Risotto (see recipe 50), adding the mushrooms 5 minutes before the end of the cooking period.

SQUASH RISOTTO

❧ SERVES 2 • PREPARATION: 20 MINUTES • COOKING: 30 MINUTES ❧

Heat 1 knob of butter in a frying pan and cook 1 chopped shallot (or onion) until soft. Add 250 g (8 oz) of puréed squash and season with 1 pinch of grated nutmeg, 1 pinch of powdered cinnamon, salt and pepper. Follow the steps for Classic Risotto (see recipe 50) adding the chopped shallot instead of the onion. After 10 minutes, mix in the puréed squash and continue to add hot stock. Crush 1 amaretto biscuit and sprinkle over the top of the risotto to garnish before serving.

LEEK & COTECHINO RISOTTO

⤜ SERVES 2 • PREPARATION: 20 MINUTES • COOKING: 30 MINUTES ⤛

Heat 1 tablespoon of olive oil and 1 knob of butter in a saucepan, then add 1 shallot and 2 chopped leeks (white parts only). Cook to soften then season with salt and pepper. Stir in the rice and follow the steps for Classic Risotto (see recipe 50). After 10 minutes, add 200 g (7 oz) of crumbled cotechino and continue to add hot chicken stock. (Note: if you cannot get hold of cotechino, use some coarse sausagemeat, browned off in a saucepan before adding to the risotto.

POTATO GNOCCHI

❧ **SERVES 6** • PREPARATION: 30 MINUTES • COOKING: A FEW MINUTES ❧

1 kg (2 lb) potatoes for mashing
250 g (8 oz) plain flour
1 egg
salt, grated nutmeg

IN ADVANCE:
Wash the potatoes, cook for 40 minutes in boiling salted water (or steam) then drain and remove the skins.

1 2
3 4

1	Mash the peeled potatoes and leave to cool.	2	Make a well in the potato and pour in three-quarters of the flour, the egg, salt and a pinch of nutmeg.	
3	Mix the ingredients, working from the centre outwards. Incorporate the remaining flour to give a smooth and even mixture.	4	Flour your hands and form the potato into long rolls about 1.5 cm (¾ in) thick then cut them into mini log shapes about 2 cm (1 in) in length.	➤

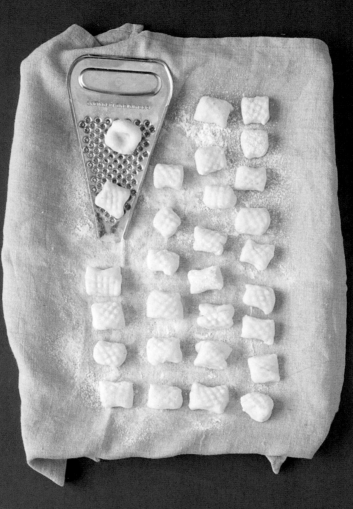

	Lightly press the gnocchi on the back of a grater to form indentations (which help the sauce to cling) then place on a lightly floured tea towel.

5

TIPS
❊

☞ Don't prepare your gnocchi too long in advance (maximum 4 hours), otherwise they will become wet and sticky! If you have any left over, keep in a cool place in an oiled dish then quickly reheat in boiling water (do not keep them for longer than 24 hours).

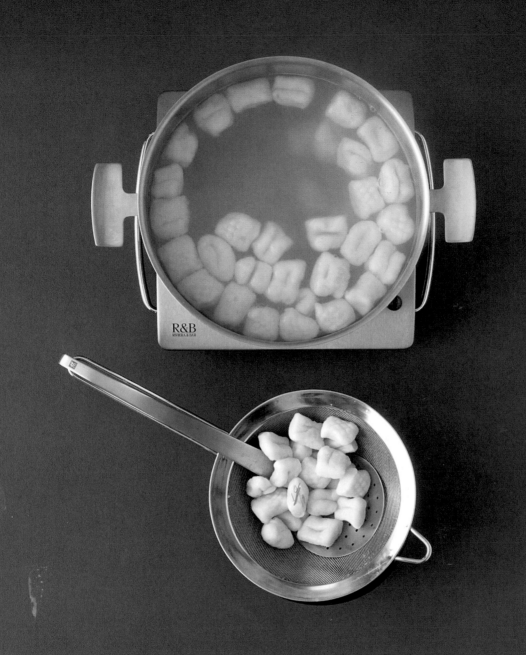

		FLAVOURINGS
6	Bring a large pan of salted water to the boil. Add the gnocchi in two batches. They are cooked as soon as they rise up to the surface: remove them immediately with a slotted spoon.	✧ with sage or cinnamon-flavoured butter (60–100 g/ 2½–3½ oz) and 60 g (2½ oz) grated Parmesan. ✧ with Tomato Sauce (see recipe 40), and using a large pat of butter at the end in place of the oil. ✧ with Bolognaise Sauce (see recipe 36). ✧ with 150 g (5 oz) Gorgonzola, melted with a little cream or milk.

ROMAN-STYLE GNOCCHI

⇻ **SERVES 6** • PREPARATION: 50 MINUTES • COOKING: 40 MINUTES ⇺

1 litre (1¾ pints) milk
250 g (8 oz) fine semolina flour
150 g (5 oz) butter

salt
75 g (3 oz) freshly grated Parmesan
2 egg yolks

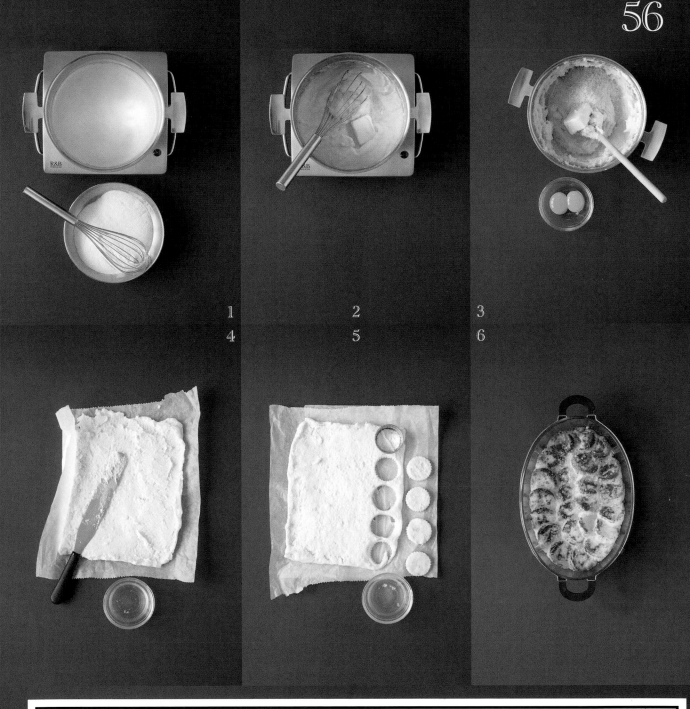

1	Bring the milk to the boil then tip in the semolina, stirring with a whisk.	2	Add 20 g (¾ oz) butter and the salt. Simmer gently for 20 minutes, stirring.	3	Off the heat, add 50 g (2 oz) butter and 50 g (2 oz) Parmesan. Stir in the eggs.
4	Tip out the mixture onto a damp sheet of baking paper and spread it out evenly.	5	Use a wetted 5–6-cm (2–2½-in) pastry cutter to press out rounds. Place in a greased ovenproof dish.	6	Top with the Parmesan and butter, melted. Put in the oven for 15 minutes at 200°C (400°F), Gas Mark 6.

FISH

4

Carpaccio of octopus 57
Sicilian-style swordfish 58
Baked marinated sea bream 59
Stuffed sardines 60
Baked sea bass with fennel 61

CARPACCIO OF OCTOPUS

❧ **SERVES 8–12** • PREPARATION: 40 MINUTES • COOKING: 1 HOUR • CHILLING: 8 HOURS ❧

1 octopus weighing about 2.5 kg (5 lb)
POACHING BROTH:
2 celery stalks + 2 onions + 2 carrots
½ bunch of parsley
1 bay leaf
6 peppercorns + sea salt

TO SERVE:
juice of 1 lemon
6 tablespoons olive oil
salt and pepper
250 g (8 oz) rocket
3–4 celery stalks, cut into dice

200 g (7 oz) black or green olives
½ bunch of parsley, chopped
IN ADVANCE:
Clean the octopus by emptying the head,
removing the eyes and beak and thoroughly
rinsing the suckers.

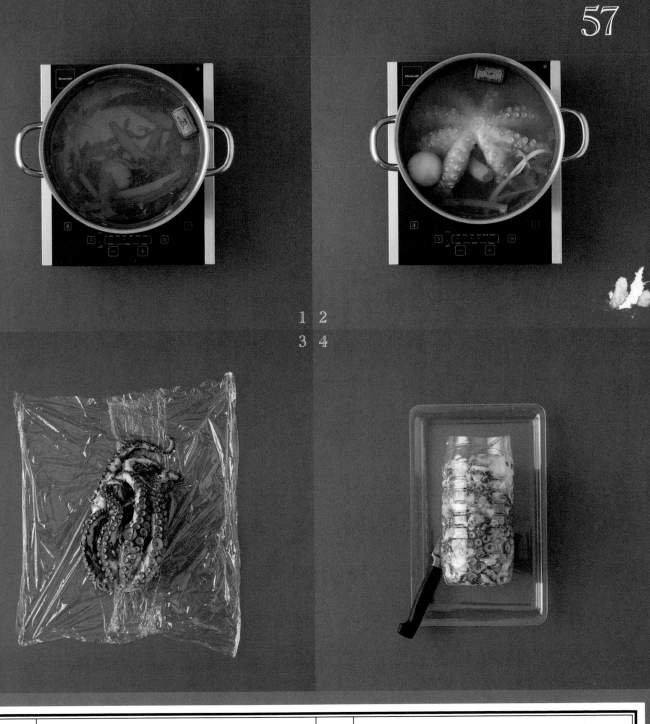

1	Bring a large stockpot of water to the boil with all the poaching ingredients and a clean cork from a bottle (it helps to tenderize the octopus).	2	Holding it by the head, gently lower in the octopus. Cook for 50–60 minutes over a medium heat. Allow to cool in the cooking water.	
3	Remove the octopus from the liquid and allow to rest a little (after cooking it will have shrunk by about two-thirds).	4	Cut off the top from a clean plastic bottle and pierce the base. Insert the octopus, packing it in firmly. Put in the fridge for 8 hours, weighted down.	➤

5	Cut the pressed octopus into thin slices.	**COOKING OCTOPUS** ❀ Octopus is cooked when you can easily insert a needle into one of the tentacles.
		DRESSING ❀ Mix the lemon juice with the olive oil, add some salt and pepper and drizzle half of it over the rocket leaves.

| 6 | Arrange the dressed rocket leaves over a large serving plate. Put the slices of octopus on top, scatter with the diced celery and the olives. Drizzle with the remaining dressing and sprinkle with the chopped parsley. | **STORING**
※

☛ Once cooked the octopus will freeze perfectly. Wrap it well in cling film. |

SICILIAN-STYLE SWORDFISH

❧ **SERVES 2** • PREPARATION: 20 MINUTES • RESTING: 1 HOUR • COOKING: 15 MINUTES ❧

3 tablespoons salted capers
2 slices of swordfish (1.5 cm/¾ in thick)
1 lemon
3 tablespoons olive oil, plus extra for cooking and greasing

2 anchovy fillets
75 g (3 oz) homemade breadcrumbs
1 garlic clove
1 tablespoon oregano

IN ADVANCE:
Rinse then chop the capers (no need for more salt in this recipe). Preheat the oven to 180°C (350°F), Gas Mark 4.

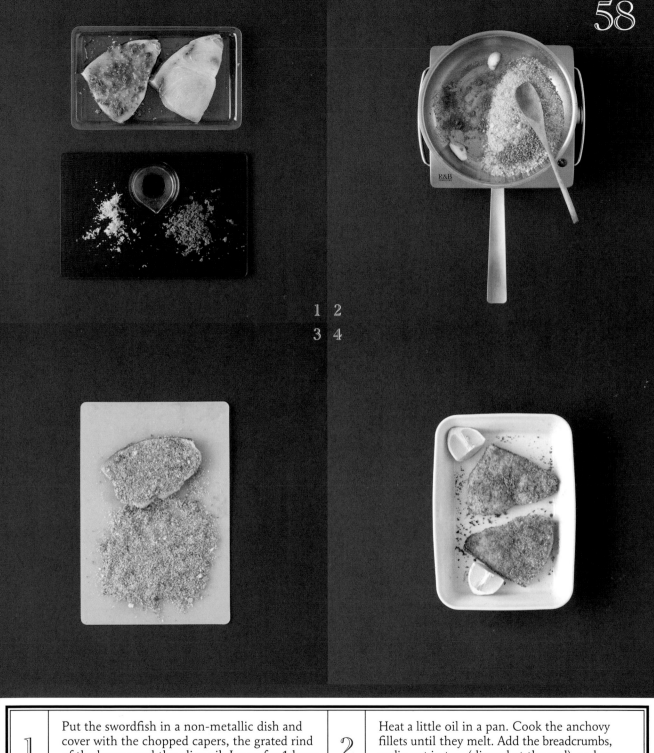

1 2
3 4

1	Put the swordfish in a non-metallic dish and cover with the chopped capers, the grated rind of the lemon and the olive oil. Leave for 1 hour to marinate.	2	Heat a little oil in a pan. Cook the anchovy fillets until they melt. Add the breadcrumbs, garlic, cut in two (discard at the end), and oregano. Stir for 1 minute over a low heat.
3	Coat the fish with the breadcrumb mixture, transfer to an oiled baking dish and drizzle over a little olive oil.	4	Transfer to the oven and cook for 15 minutes. Serve with a squeeze of lemon and a tomato salad or Tomato Gratin (see recipe 25).

MARINATED BAKED SEA BREAM

➤ **SERVES 4** • PREPARATION: 15 MINUTES • MARINATING: 30 MINUTES • COOKING: 20 MINUTES ➤

MARINADE:
1 small onion + 1 garlic clove
100 ml (3½ fl oz) white wine
6 flat leaf parsley stalks
2 tablespoons olive oil

2 pinches sea salt
1 sea bream weighing about 1 kg (2 lb)
(or sea bass or scorpion fish), cleaned and
scaled
150 ml (¼ pint) mineral water

10 g (½ oz) sea salt
200 g (7 oz) cherry tomatoes
IN ADVANCE:
Cut the onion for the marinade into rings
and the garlic into small pieces.

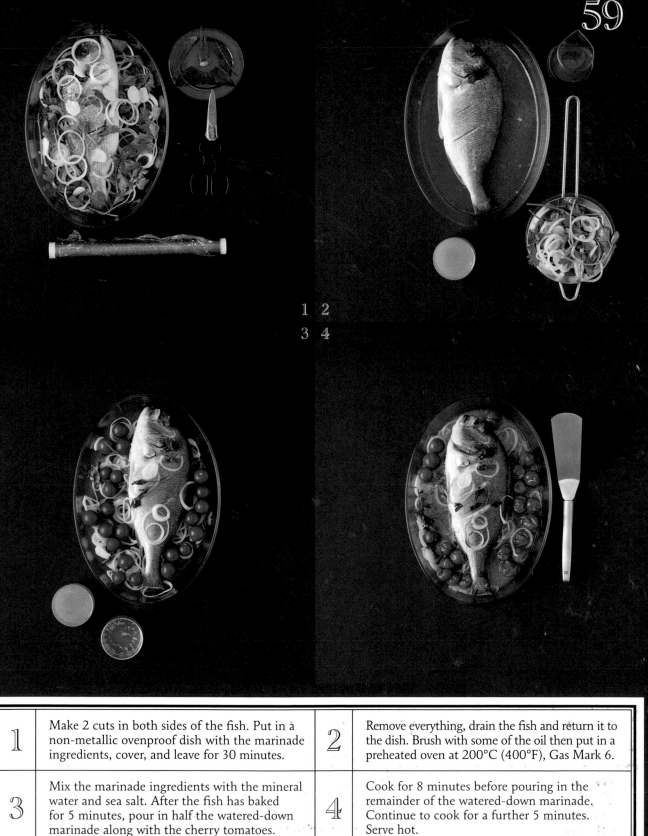

1	Make 2 cuts in both sides of the fish. Put in a non-metallic ovenproof dish with the marinade ingredients, cover, and leave for 30 minutes.	2	Remove everything, drain the fish and return it to the dish. Brush with some of the oil then put in a preheated oven at 200°C (400°F), Gas Mark 6.
3	Mix the marinade ingredients with the mineral water and sea salt. After the fish has baked for 5 minutes, pour in half the watered-down marinade along with the cherry tomatoes.	4	Cook for 8 minutes before pouring in the remainder of the watered-down marinade. Continue to cook for a further 5 minutes. Serve hot.

STUFFED SARDINES

❧ SERVES 4 • PREPARATION: 30 MINUTES • COOKING: 15 MINUTES ❧

12 really fresh medium sardines
75 g (3 oz) homemade breadcrumbs
4 anchovy fillets
20 g (¾ oz) salted capers
40 g (1½ oz) raisins

40 g (1½ oz) pine nuts
3 parsley stalks
2 mint stalks
juice of 1 small lemon and 1 orange
4 tablespoons olive oil

salt and freshly ground pepper
10–12 bay leaves
½ teaspoon sugar
1 tablespoon red wine vinegar

1 2
3 4

1	Clean and scale the sardines, then remove the heads and backbones. Rinse under running water, dry on kitchen paper then open out flat down their length.	2	Whiz the breadcrumbs in a blender with the anchovies, capers, raisins, pine nuts, herbs, rind of the lemon, and 2–3 tablespoons olive oil. Taste before adding salt.
3	Spread 1 teaspoon of the mixture on the opened sardines, pressing it down, then roll them up towards the tail.	4	Pack the rolled sardines tightly into an ovenproof dish, tucking in a bayleaf between each one. ➤

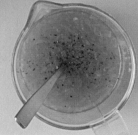

5	Mix the orange and lemon juice with the sugar, vinegar, a drizzle of olive oil, and the pepper. Pour over the prepared sardines.	**TO SAVE TIME** ❈ You can ask your fishmonger to prepare the sardines.
		TIP ❈ The sardines must be really fresh. Do not buy ready filleted ones.

6	Transfer to a preheated oven at 180°C (350°F), Gas Mark 4 for about 15 minutes. Serve warm or at room temperature with a rocket salad.	**WITH DRINKS** ❋
		Once the sardines are cooked, cut each roll in half and spear with a cocktail stick.

BAKED SEA BASS WITH FENNEL

⇜ **SERVES 2** • **PREPARATION: 15 MINUTES** • **COOKING: 15 MINUTES** ⇝

1 whole sea bass weighing about 600–700 g
(1¼–1½ lb)
2 fennel bulbs
olive oil
salt and freshly ground pepper

50 g (2 oz) fine semolina (pasta) flour or
cornflour
½ teaspoon fennel seeds
1 tablespoon reduced balsamic vinegar
(see recipe 62)

IN ADVANCE:
Preheat the oven to 200°C (400°F),
Gas Mark 6.

	TO CLEAN THE FISH	TO FILLET THE FISH
1	❖ Scale: Hold the fish by its tail and scrape off the scales using a firm-bladed knife. Rinse. ❖ Clean: Open up the belly and remove all the intestines. ❖ Trim: Cut off all fins and barbs, working from the head towards the tail.	❖ Bone: Dry the fish. Place on a chopping board with the cleaned belly towards you. Place a hand on top. Using a very sharp filleting knife, make an incision underneath and above the entire length of the dorsal spine, starting from the head. Slip the blade under the backbone and gently remove the fillet. Ease out the backbone and remove the second fillet.

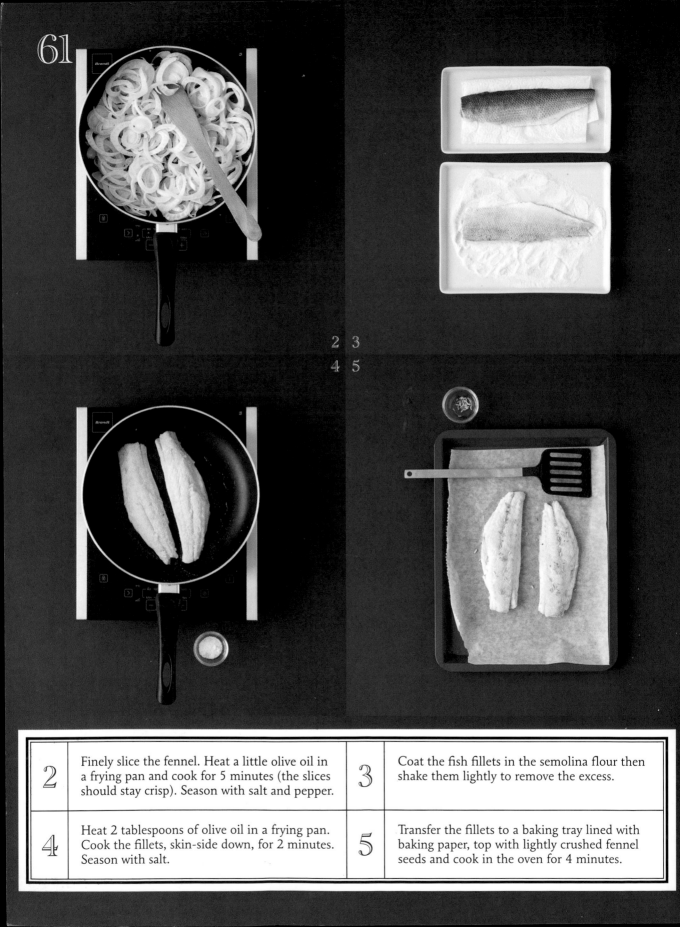

2 3
4 5

2	Finely slice the fennel. Heat a little olive oil in a frying pan and cook for 5 minutes (the slices should stay crisp). Season with salt and pepper.	3	Coat the fish fillets in the semolina flour then shake them lightly to remove the excess.
4	Heat 2 tablespoons of olive oil in a frying pan. Cook the fillets, skin-side down, for 2 minutes. Season with salt.	5	Transfer the fillets to a baking tray lined with baking paper, top with lightly crushed fennel seeds and cook in the oven for 4 minutes.

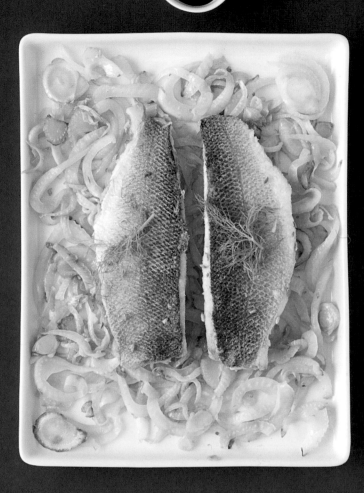

| 6 | Serve the bass on the fennel slices with the reduced balsamic vinegar drizzled on top. | **TIPS**
❀

☛ Try to buy line-caught bass for preference. You can always ask your fishmonger to clean and fillet the whole fish for you. |

MEAT

5

IN SLICES

Carpaccio of beef.................................... 62
Veal in tuna sauce................................... 63
Fillet of beef 64

PAN-FRIED

Milan-style veal escalopes............................. 65
Saltimbocca... 66
Chicken & ricotta parcel 67

IN SAUCE

Guineafowl in pepper sauce........................... 68
Milan-style osso buco................................ 69
Veal stew with polenta............................... 70
Polenta 71

CARPACCIO OF BEEF

⋟ **SERVES 6 • PREPARATION: 30 MINUTES** ⋞

6 tablespoons balsamic vinegar
700 g (1¼ lb) best quality beef fillet
(ask for the centre cut)
olive oil

salt and freshly ground pepper
150 g (5 oz) rocket leaves
75 g (3 oz) Parmesan shavings
75 g (3 oz) black olives

IN ADVANCE:
Put the vinegar in a small saucepan over
a medium heat and cook to reduce to a
syrupy consistency.

1 2
3 4

1	Cut the beef into very thin slices with a well-sharpened knife.	2	Cut out 12 squares of baking paper. Place 4–5 slices of beef side by side on half of the sheets.
3	Cover with the other 6 squares of paper then bat out the meat until very flat using a meat mallet.	4	Use kitchen scissors to cut the excess paper from around the meat so that they resemble dinner plates. ➤

	Peel off the top sheet and invert the meat on a plate so that the second sheet of paper is uppermost. Peel that off too. Use a pastry brush to brush the beef slices with a little olive oil.	**TIP** ☞ It's easier to cut the meat into very thin slices if you put the piece in the freezer, wrapped tightly in cling film, before cutting it.
5		

6	At the point of serving, season the beef with salt and pepper. Top with some rocket leaves dressed with 2 tablespoons of olive oil, some salt and some pepper. Garnish with Parmesan shavings, black olives and a drizzle of reduced balsamic vinegar.	**IN ADVANCE** ❈ You can make the carpaccio ahead of serving if you cover it well with cling film and keep in the fridge. **CARPACCIO EXPRESS** ❈ ☛ Ask your butcher to prepare the thin slices on his bacon slicer, or buy beef ready-sliced for carpaccio.

VEAL IN TUNA SAUCE

❖ SERVES 6–8 • PREPARATION: 20 MINUTES • COOKING: 40 MINUTES ❖

1 onion
1 carrot
1 celery stalk
several flat leaf parsley stalks
1 kg (2 lb) boneless veal topside

TUNA SAUCE:
300 g (10 oz) tuna in oil, drained
6 anchovy fillets
30 g (1 oz) capers (salted for preference)
1 handful of flat leaf parsley

100 g (3½ oz) mayonnaise
salt and freshly ground pepper

IN ADVANCE:
Peel and chop all the vegetables and parsley.

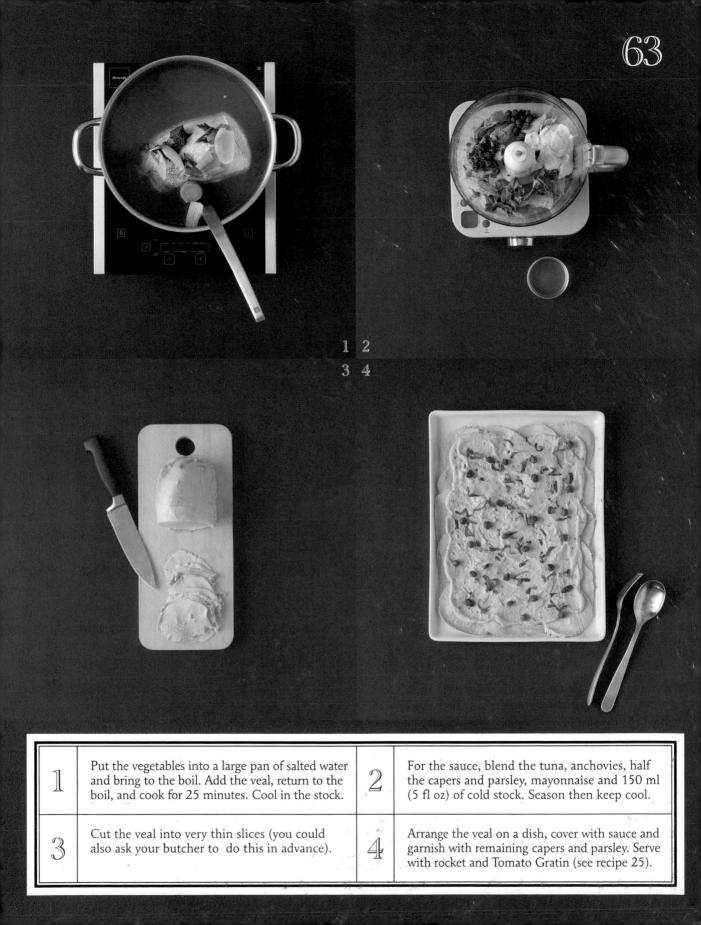

1	Put the vegetables into a large pan of salted water and bring to the boil. Add the veal, return to the boil, and cook for 25 minutes. Cool in the stock.	2	For the sauce, blend the tuna, anchovies, half the capers and parsley, mayonnaise and 150 ml (5 fl oz) of cold stock. Season then keep cool.
3	Cut the veal into very thin slices (you could also ask your butcher to do this in advance).	4	Arrange the veal on a dish, cover with sauce and garnish with remaining capers and parsley. Serve with rocket and Tomato Gratin (see recipe 25).

FILLET OF BEEF

❖ **SERVES 2** • PREPARATION: 10 MINUTES • MARINADE: 1 HOUR • COOKING: 5 MINUTES ❖

balsamic vinegar
300 g (10 oz) beef fillet (1.5 cm/¾ in thick)
olive oil
3 rosemary stalks

salt flakes and freshly ground pepper
100 g (3½ oz) rocket leaves
20 g (¾ oz) Parmesan shavings

IN ADVANCE:
Reduce 4 tablespoons of balsamic vinegar
(see recipe 62).

1 2
3 4

1	Brush the beef with olive oil and sprinkle with rosemary. Place in a dish, cover with cling film and leave to marinate for 1 hour at room temperature.	2	Preheat the grill or a heavy, ridged pan and cook the meat for 2 minutes on each side (longer if you like it more cooked). Generously season with salt and pepper and keep warm.
3	Pour 1 or 2 tablespoons water into the pan, scraping up the bits stuck to the base, and allow the juices to reduce.	4	Cut the meat into 8 pieces. Serve with the rocket leaves dressed with the meat juices and the balsamic vinegar, and the Parmesan.

MILAN-STYLE VEAL ESCALOPES

➤ **SERVES 2** • PREPARATION: 20 MINUTES • COOKING: 5 MINUTES ➤

2 veal escalopes
4 or 5 slices of fresh bread (soft batch, crusts removed), made into crumbs
1 egg

10 g (½ oz) butter
2 tablespoons olive oil
1 lemon
salt

IN ADVANCE:
Use a meat mallet to flatten the veal to 3–4 mm (⅛ in) thick between 2 sheets of baking paper. Reduce the bread to crumbs in a mixer.

1	Beat the egg in a shallow dish and spread the breadcrumbs on a sheet of baking paper.	2	Dip both sides of the escalopes first in egg then in breadcrumbs, pressing them in firmly to make sure they stick.
3	Melt the butter with the oil in a frying pan and fry the escalopes until both sides are golden-brown.	4	Dry the escalopes on kitchen paper, season with salt and serve hot or cold with a lemon quarter and tomato salad.

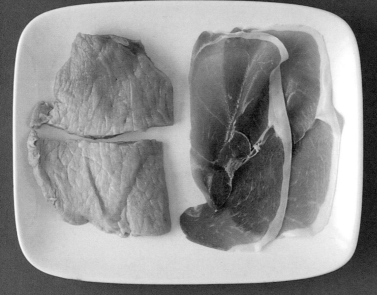

SALTIMBOCCA

❖ **SERVES 2** • PREPARATION: 15 MINUTES • COOKING: 8 MINUTES ❖

2 veal escalopes, weighing about 150 g
(5 oz) each
2 thin slices of Parma ham
4 sage leaves

1 tablespoon olive oil
30 g (1 oz) butter
500 ml (1 pint) dry white wine or water
pinch of salt

TIP:
If you don't have a meat mallet, bat out
the meat with the base of a small heavy
saucepan.

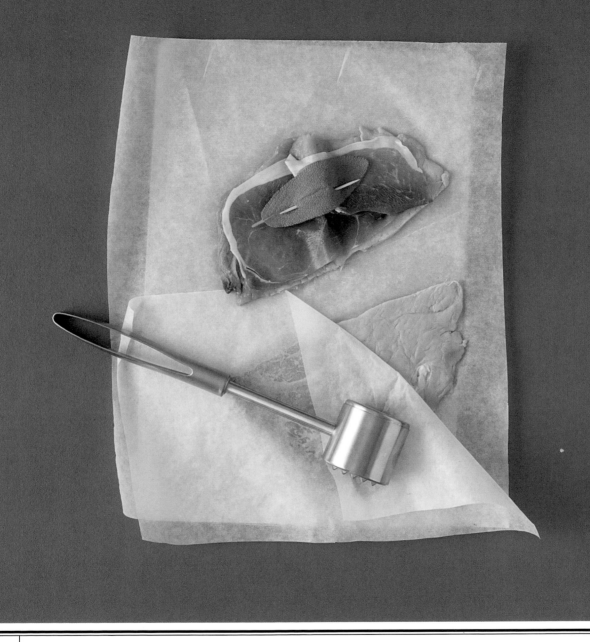

1. Place the escalopes between 2 sheets of baking parchment and use a meat mallet to gently bat them out very thinly. Place ½ slice of ham and 1 sage leaf on each escalope and secure with a cocktail stick.

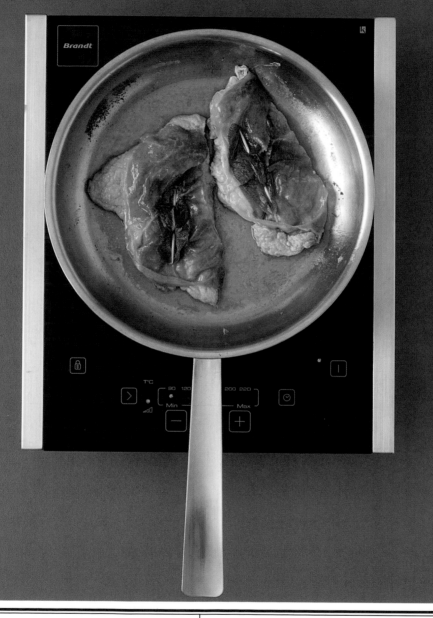

2	Heat the oil and two-thirds of the butter in a frying pan over a medium-high heat. Cook the escalopes, first on the ham side then on the second side (about 5 minutes in total). Remove and keep warm while you make the sauce.

TO MAKE THE SAUCE
❈

☛ Pour the wine (or water) into the frying pan, scraping the caramelized bits on the base. Allow to boil for 1 minute then add the remaining butter and a pinch of salt.

3

Pour the sauce over the escalopes and serve
with a salad of rocket leaves or with a selection
of seasonal vegetables.

CHICKEN & RICOTTA PARCEL

✣ **SERVES 6** • PREPARATION: 20 MINUTES • COOKING: 40 MINUTES ✣

500 g (1 lb) chicken breasts
500 g (1 lb) ricotta
50 g (2 oz) freshly grated Parmesan
2 egg yolks
salt and freshly ground pepper

3 pinches of grated nutmeg
10–12 slices Parma ham or speck (smoked cured ham)
knob of butter + 1 tablespoon olive oil
sage leaves

50 ml (2 fl oz) dry white wine
IN ADVANCE:
Remove any fat from the chicken and finely chop (easiest in a food-processor). Preheat the oven to 180°C (350°F), Gas Mark 4.

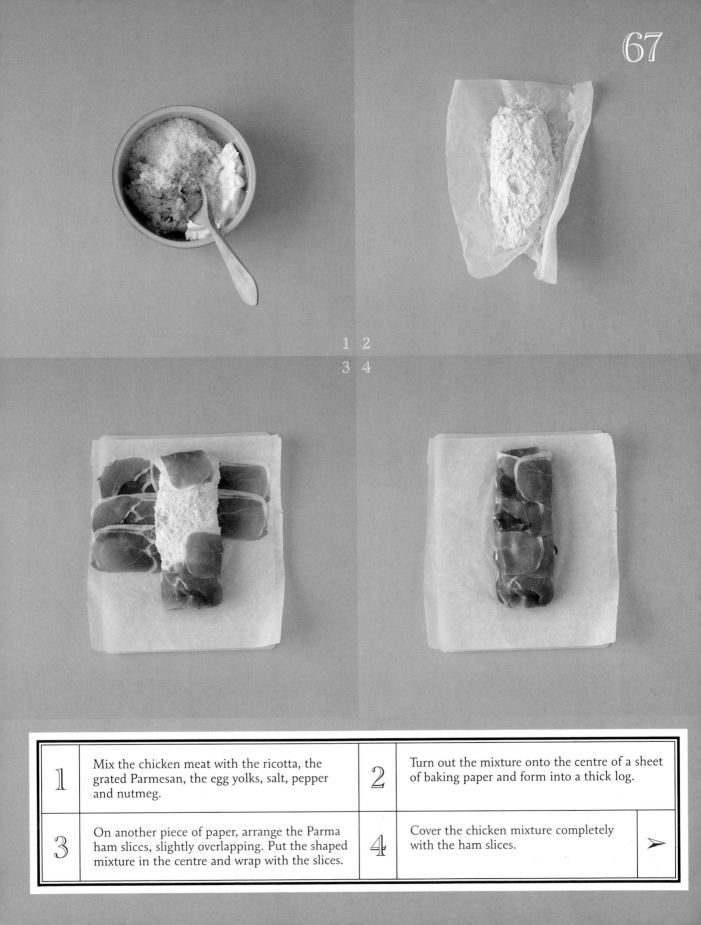

1	Mix the chicken meat with the ricotta, the grated Parmesan, the egg yolks, salt, pepper and nutmeg.	2	Turn out the mixture onto the centre of a sheet of baking paper and form into a thick log.	
3	On another piece of paper, arrange the Parma ham slices, slightly overlapping. Put the shaped mixture in the centre and wrap with the slices.	4	Cover the chicken mixture completely with the ham slices.	➤

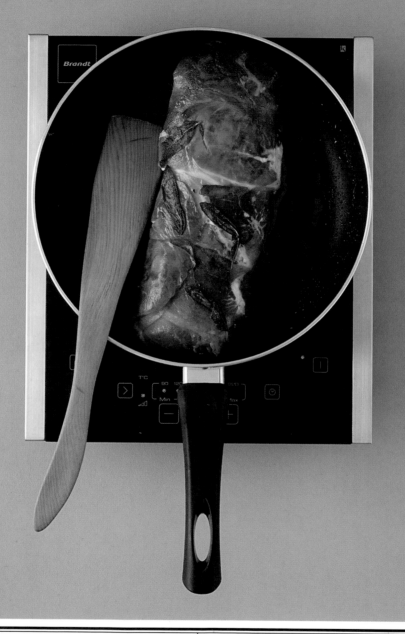

5	Heat the butter and the oil in a large frying pan with the sage leaves. Place the wrapped parcel in the pan and brown on all sides.	**ALTERNATIVE** ❋ ☛ You can completely cook the parcel in the frying pan, covered with a lid or aluminium foil, over a low heat.

		VARIATION
		❈
6	Transfer the parcel to a baking tray and continue to cook in the oven for 30 minutes. After 10 minutes, pour in the white wine, allow it to evaporate, then cover the tray with aluminium foil. Serve cut into slices, with vegetables.	Use minced veal instead of chicken.

GUINEAFOWL IN PEPPER SAUCE

⇌ SERVES 4 • PREPARATION: 30 MINUTES • COOKING: 1 HOUR ⇌

1 guineafowl weighing at least 1 kg (2 lb)
100 g lardo di Colonnata (cured pork fat)
or pancetta, sliced finely
2 rosemary stalks
20 g (¾ oz) butter + 2 tablespoons olive oil
2 bay leaves + 4 garlic cloves, chopped small

salt and freshly ground pepper
150 ml (5 fl oz) dry white wine
PEPPER SAUCE:
200 g (7 oz) chicken livers
giblets from the guineafowl
100 g (3½ oz) sopressa (a cured sausage)

1 lemon
2 garlic cloves
150 ml (5 fl oz) olive oil
150 ml (5 fl oz) dry white wine
salt and freshly ground pepper
1 bunch of flat leaf parsley, chopped

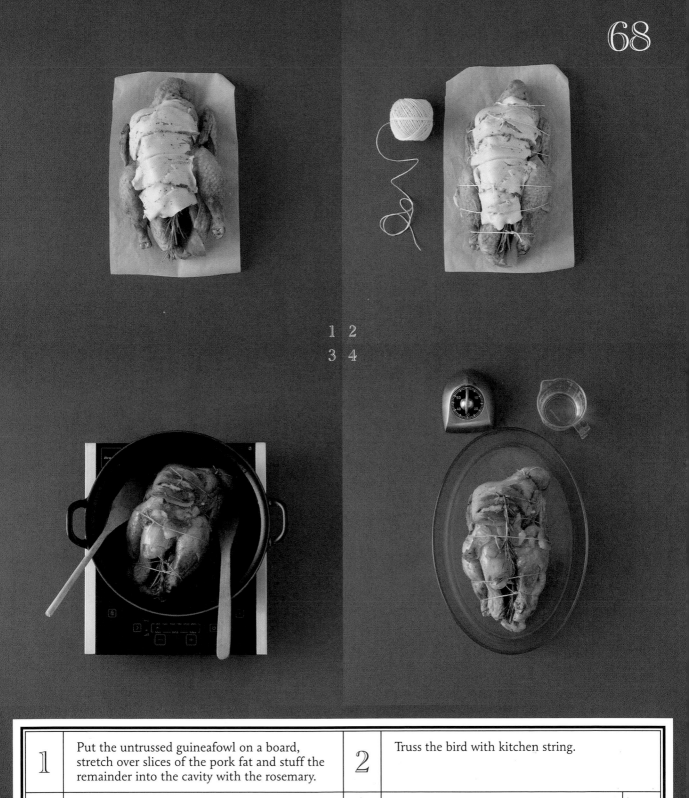

1	Put the untrussed guineafowl on a board, stretch over slices of the pork fat and stuff the remainder into the cavity with the rosemary.	2	Truss the bird with kitchen string.
3	Heat the butter and the oil in a large casserole, add the bay leaves and garlic and brown the guineafowl on all sides. Season with salt and pepper. Drain and discard the fat from the pan.	4	Transfer the bird to the oven at 200°C (400°F), Gas Mark 6 for 40 minutes. After 10 minutes, pour over the wine, then, at regular intervals, a little water. ➤

5 6
7 8

5	To make the sauce, trim the chicken livers and giblets and chop the sopressa. Grate the lemon rind and squeeze the juice.	6	Put all these ingredients, except the lemon juice, in a food-processor with 1 garlic clove. Finely chop.
7	Heat the olive oil in a saucepan with the second garlic clove (discarding it as soon as the oil is hot). Add the chicken liver mixture and brown, stirring.	8	Add the wine and juices from the guineafowl. Add a little salt and plenty of pepper. Cook gently for 10 minutes, add the lemon juice and parsley and cook for a further 5 minutes.

9	To serve, cut the guineafowl into 4, coat with the pepper sauce and accompany with polenta (see recipe 72).	**VARIATION** ❈ ☛ Instead of the sopressa you can use 8 anchovy fillets. For a slightly more tart-tasting sauce, use 4–5 tablespoons of vinegar instead of lemon juice.

MILAN-STYLE OSSO BUCO

⇥ **SERVES 4** • PREPARATION: 30 MINUTES • COOKING: 1 HOUR 30 MINUTES ⇤

2 onions
4 slices of shin of veal, about 5 cm
(2 in) thick
40 g (1½ oz) plain flour
4 tablespoons olive oil

65 g (2½ oz) butter
150 ml (5 fl oz) dry white wine
salt and freshly ground pepper
200–300 ml (7–10 fl oz) meat stock

GREMOLATA:
1 garlic clove
1 bunch of flat leaf parsley, 1 unwaxed lemon
IN ADVANCE:
Chop the onions very finely.

1	Make 3 small cuts around the sides of the shin slices so that they remain flat during cooking, then lightly dust with flour.	2	Heat half the oil and a third of the butter in a large casserole. Add the onions and cook very gently for 20 minutes. Remove and set aside.
3	Add the remaining oil and another third of the butter to the pan. Brown the veal slices for 5 minutes on each side. Return the onions.	4	Pour in the white wine, leave to evaporate for 6–7 minutes, season with salt and pepper and add half a glass of stock. ➤

5 6
7 8

5	Cover the casserole and cook over a very low heat for 1 hour 20 minutes (or in the oven in a shallow dish, covered with a sheet of buttered aluminium foil at 180°C/350°F, Gas Mark 4).	6	As it cooks, turn the meat from time to time and keep topping up with a little stock as the sauce thickens.
7	To make the gremolata, crush the garlic then finely chop the flat leaf parsley with the garlic and the rind of half the lemon.	8	The meat is cooked when it falls off the bones. Remove the pieces and blend the sauce with the remaining butter and half the gremolata.

9

Replace the meat in the casserole and reheat gently for 2 minutes. Serve sprinkled with the remaining gremolata, accompanied with Saffron Risotto (see recipe 51).

VARIATION

※

Add 150 g (5 oz) of peeled, deseeded and chopped tomatoes before covering the casserole in step 5.

TIP

※

☞ For the most succulent flavour, buy milk-fed veal.

VEAL STEW WITH POLENTA

❧ SERVES 6 • PREPARATION: 30 MINUTES • COOKING: 1 HOUR 30 MINUTES ❧

1.5 kg (3 lb) stewing veal
2 onions
2 carrots
2 celery stalks
1 garlic clove

20 g (¾ oz) butter
4 tablespoons olive oil
6 sage leaves
1 rosemary stalk
100 ml (3½ fl oz) dry white wine

800 g (1 lb 12 oz) tinned chopped tomatoes
meat stock (optional)
salt and freshly ground pepper
Polenta made with 500 g (1 lb) cornmeal
(see recipe 72)

1	Cut the meat into 5-cm (2-in) cubes and finely chop all the vegetables.	2	Heat the butter and oil in a large casserole and seal the meat pieces in 2 batches, for 5 minutes each batch. Remove and keep warm.
3	Add the vegetables to the casserole and cook for a few minutes.	4	Return the meat with the herbs, allow to brown, then pour in the wine and stir until it evaporates. ➤

| 5 | Reduce the sauce before adding the chopped tomatoes. Cover the pan and leave to gently simmer over a very low heat for 1 hour. If the sauce reduces too much, add a little stock or water. | **VARIATION**
❋
For a white veal stew, use all stock instead of tomatoes. You can also equally use beef, lamb or chine of pork in this recipe and add spices or other herbs. |

6   Season with salt and pepper at the end of cooking and serve with hot polenta.

❋

Accompany with a selection of seasonal vegetables.

POLENTA

❖ COOKING: 5 MINUTES FOR PRECOOKED POLENTA, 45 MINUTES FOR CORNMEAL ❖

2 litres (3½ pints) water (use 2.5 litres/4 pints for wetter polenta or 1.5 litres/2½ pints for a firm polenta)

salt
500 g (1 lb) yellow cornmeal for polenta (either precooked or uncooked)

QUANTITIES:
Allow 4–5 times the amount of water to polenta.

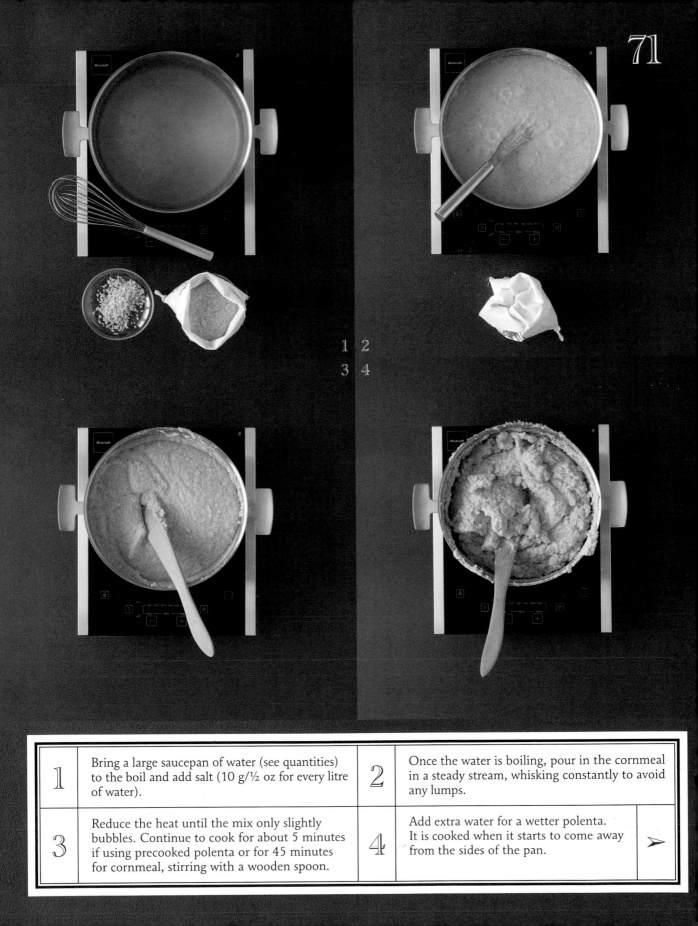

1	Bring a large saucepan of water (see quantities) to the boil and add salt (10 g/½ oz for every litre of water).	2	Once the water is boiling, pour in the cornmeal in a steady stream, whisking constantly to avoid any lumps.
3	Reduce the heat until the mix only slightly bubbles. Continue to cook for about 5 minutes if using precooked polenta or for 45 minutes for cornmeal, stirring with a wooden spoon.	4	Add extra water for a wetter polenta. It is cooked when it starts to come away from the sides of the pan.

	TO SERVE	VARIATION
5	Put the hot polenta on a wooden board to serve, or press into a dampened mould to give a shape. A wetter polenta is served with a spoon. Polenta can be served with meat or fish in a sauce, with cheese, cooked meats, pan-fried mushrooms, and so forth.	For a lighter polenta, use half water and half milk. You can add a knob of butter or grated Parmesan. **SUGGESTION** Just before the end of cooking, add some cooked mushrooms, chopped olives or sun-dried tomatoes.

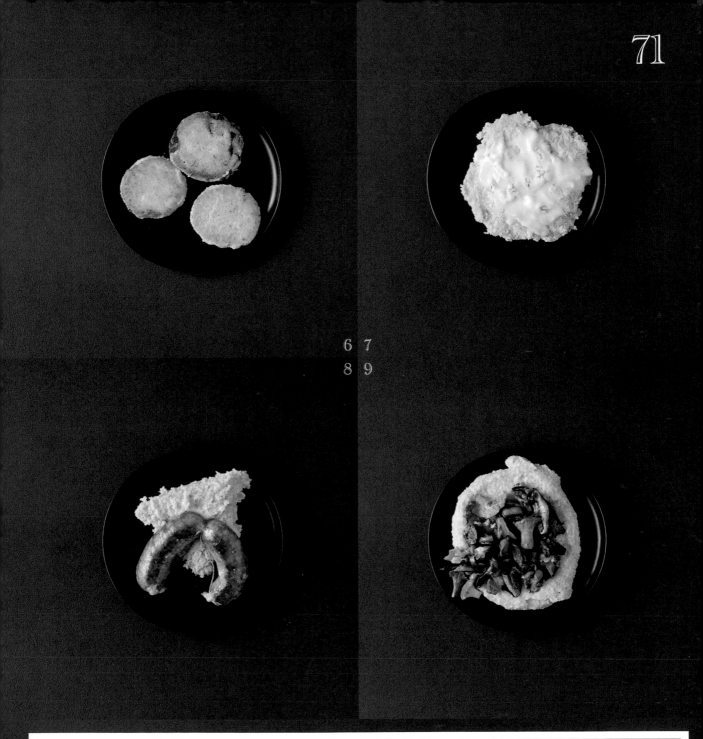

6 7
8 9

	POLENTA GRATIN			POLENTA WITH GORGONZOLA
6	Allow the polenta to cool, cut into pieces and reheat in the oven or in a frying pan with a little butter.		7	Top the hot polenta with Gorgonzola or other strongly flavoured cheese.
	POLENTA WITH SAUSAGES			POLENTA WITH MUSHROOMS
8	Serve the polenta with fried sausages or with sopressa (a soft cured sausage).		9	Serve with pan-fried mixed wild mushrooms (see recipe 34).

DESSERTS

6

CREAMY

Tiramisu 72
Panna cotta 73
Sabayon 74
Semifreddo 75

CAKES & TARTS

Chocolate amaretti cake 76
Sweet shortcrust pastry 77
Ricotta, pine nut & raisin tart 78
Red fruit tartlets 79
Auntie's rice cake 80
Baked peaches 81
Rich pandoro dessert 82

TIRAMISU

⟫ SERVES 4 • PREPARATION: 30 MINUTES • CHILLING: 2 HOURS MINIMUM ⟪

3 small, really fresh eggs
3 tablespoons white sugar
3 tablespoons dry marsala

250 g (8 oz) chilled mascarpone
100 g (3½ oz) Pavesini biscuits or
sponge fingers (ladyfingers)

4 shots hot espresso
1 tablespoon cocoa powder
1 pinch of salt

1 2
3 4

1	Separate the eggs.	2	Use a hand-held electric whisk to beat the egg yolks with the sugar until light and creamy.	
3	Add the marsala and mascarpone to the egg mixture, a little at a time.	4	Whisk for a few more minutes until you have a smooth, thick cream. Put in the fridge to keep cold.	➤

| 5 | 6 |
| 7 | 8 |

5	Whisk the egg whites with the salt into firm peaks.	6	Use the whisk to gently incorporate the beaten egg whites into the mascarpone mixture.
7	Spread 2 tablespoons of the mixture in the base of a shallow-sided square or oblong dish. Quickly soak the biscuits in the hot coffee and arrange a layer on top of the cream mixture.	8	Cover the biscuits with more cream and build up 2 further layers in this way, finishing with a layer of cream. Chill in the fridge for a minimum of 2 hours.

9	To serve, dust the top with the cocoa powder sifted through a tea strainer.	**TIP** ❀
		☛ Eat tiramisu within 24 hours because it contains raw eggs.

VARIATION ❀	**SUMMER TIRAMISU** ❀
You can make the dessert with slices of sponge cake that has gone a little dry (build up 2 layers only).	Instead of coffee, use strawberry coulis (see recipe 73), thinned with a little orange juice, and decorate with red berries before serving.

PANNA COTTA

⤞ SERVES 8 • PREPARATION: 15 MINUTES • COOKING: 10 MINUTES • CHILLING: ABOUT 3 HOURS ⤝

1 litre (1¾ pints) double or whipping cream
(or crème fleurette, if you can find it)
1 vanilla pod, split in two

grated rind of 1 unwaxed lemon
3 tablespoons vanilla-flavoured powder for
making crème caramel (sold in sachets)

TIP:
If you can't find the vanilla powder, use
3 tablespoons sugar and 10 g (½ oz)
gelatine or 1 level teaspoon of agar-agar.

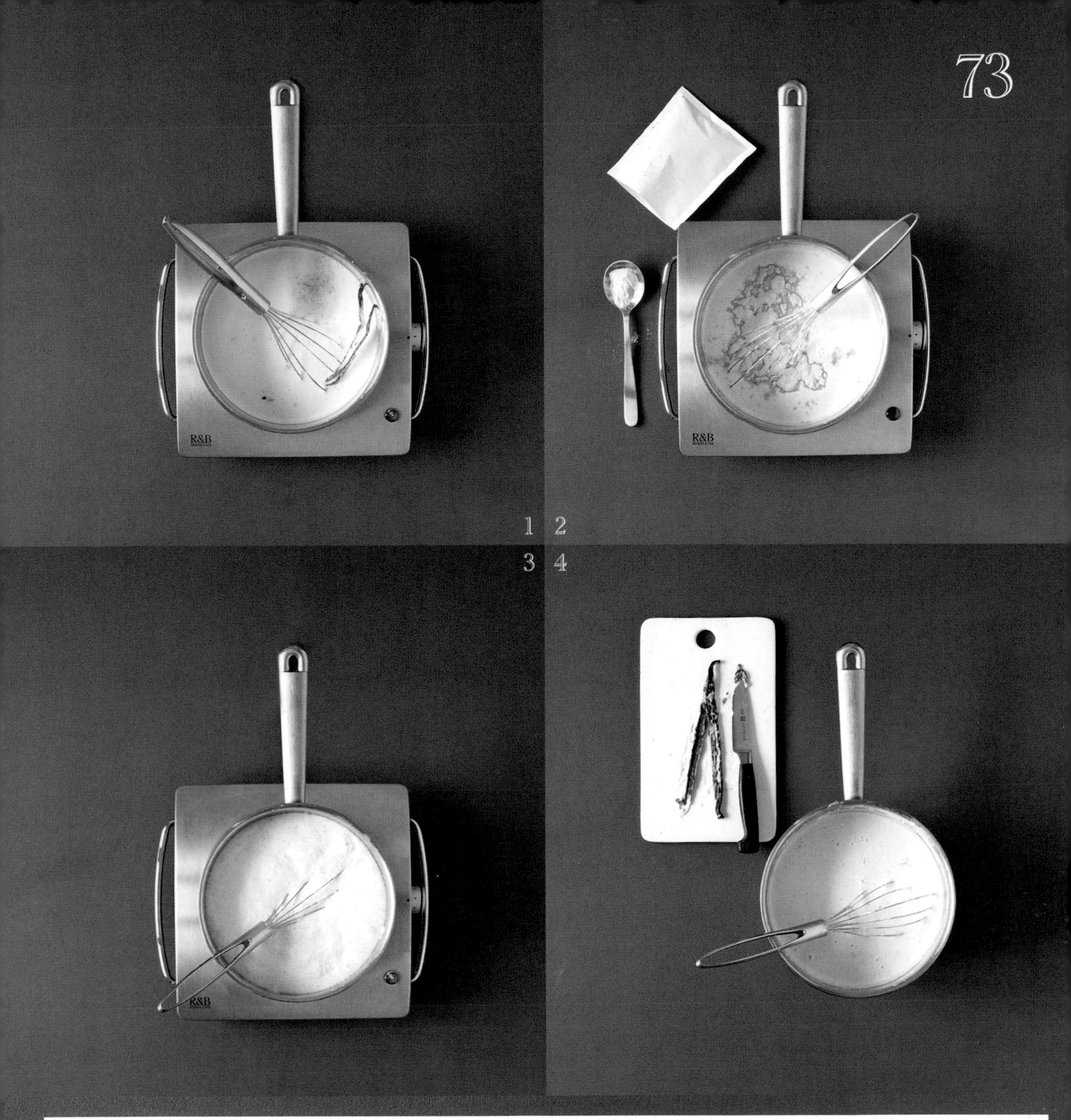

1	Put the cream with the vanilla pod and the lemon zest in a saucepan and gently heat, stirring, for 3 minutes.	2	Sprinkle in the sachet of vanilla powder, whisking continuously.
3	Continue to stir with the whisk until the cream starts to bubble.	4	Remove from the heat, remove the vanilla pod and scrape any remaining seeds into the cream. Leave to cool for 5 minutes, stirring from time to time. ➢

| 5 | Rinse 8 moulds or ramekin dishes with water but don't dry them; this will make it easier to slip out the desserts. Pour the cream mixture into a jug then fill the moulds. Leave to cool completely before covering with cling film and chilling in the fridge for 3 hours. | **VARIATION**
❋
You can flavour your panna cotta with a little marsala or rum, with flower waters (rose- or orange-flower), with fruit syrup, infusions or spices. For a coffee-flavoured version, add 50 g (2 oz) sugar and 3 teaspoons of instant coffee granules. |

6

To turn out the desserts, run the point of a knife round the rims, put a plate on top and quickly invert, giving each one a sharp shake.

TO SERVE

❋

For a fresh coulis of strawberries (or other red fruits), blend 500 g (1 lb) strawberries with 3 tablespoons sugar and a squeeze of lemon juice. Rub everything through a fine-mesh sieve, adding a little water if necessary to give a pouring consistency. Otherwise, try serving with a drizzle of caramel or a reduction of balsamic vinegar (see recipe 62).

SABAYON

❧ **SERVES 6** • PREPARATION: 15 MINUTES • COOKING: 10 MINUTES ❧

6 egg yolks
100 g (3½ oz) granulated cane sugar
150 ml (5 fl oz) dry marsala

ALTERNATIVE:
Mix the chilled sabayon with 200 ml (7 fl oz)
whipped cream and serve with fresh fruits.

1	Mix the egg yolks, sugar and marsala in a bowl and set over a saucepan of barely simmering hot water.	2	Whisk everything together using a hand-held electric whisk.
3	After about 5 minutes you should have a thick mousse-like mixture.	4	Serve the sabayon hot or warm with biscuits. To chill it (see alternative), plunge the bowl in iced water and stir frequently.

SEMIFREDDO

⇢ SERVES 10 • PREPARATION: 30 MINUTES • FREEZING: 6 HOURS ⇠

200 g (7 oz) almond torrone (nougat)
100 g (3½ oz) plain dark chocolate
(70% cocoa solids)
500 ml (17 fl oz) chilled double or
whipping cream

1 sabayon (see recipe 74)
IN ADVANCE:
Oil a large loaf tin (or 10 individual
moulds) and line with cling film.

RED FRUIT VERSION:
Mix 400 g (14 oz) mixed red berries and
200 ml (7 fl oz) whipped cream with the
cooled sabayon.

1 2
3 4

1	Roughly chop the torrone and chocolate.	2	Whip the cream and fold gently into the cooled sabayon.
3	Spread one-third of the nougat and chocolate in the lined mould and cover with one-third of the cream. Repeat twice. Freeze for 6 hours.	4	Remove the semifreddo from the freezer about 10 minutes before serving. Quickly dip the mould into hot water and turn out the semifreddo.

CHOCOLATE AMARETTI CAKE

⇝ SERVES 6–8 • PREPARATION: 30 MINUTES • COOKING: 25 MINUTES ⇜

100 g (3½ oz) plain dark chocolate
(70% cocoa solids)
100 g (3½ oz) butter + an extra knob
70 g amaretti (look for the crunchy variety
for preference)

3 eggs
150 g caster sugar
50 g (2 oz) plain flour
¼ teaspoon baking powder
65 g (2½ oz) toasted almonds

GANACHE:
100 g (3½ oz) plain dark chocolate
100 ml (3½ fl oz) single or whipping cream
IN ADVANCE:
Heat the oven to 180°C (350°F), Gas Mark 4.

1 2
3 4

1	Break up the chocolate and put in a bowl with the butter cut into pieces. Set the bowl over a saucepan of barely simmering hot water.	2	Whiz the amaretti in a food-processor or crush to crumbs with a rolling pin.
3	Generously grease a 20-cm (8-in) round cake tin with the knob of butter. Use the amaretti crumbs to line the base and the sides. Chill in the fridge.	4	Whisk the eggs and the sugar until they are light and creamy.

5	Sift in the flour with the baking powder, incorporate with the whisk, then add in the cooled melted chocolate.	6	Pour into the mould and transfer to the oven for 25 minutes. Insert the point of a knife into the middle of the cake: it should come out clean.
7	To make the ganache, melt the chocolate and cream in a bowl set over a saucepan of barely simmering hot water.	8	Allow the cake to cool for 5 minutes before turning out on a wire rack. Spread the ganache over the surface using a plastic spatula.

| 9 | Decorate the cake with the toasted almonds, roughly chopped. | **TIP**
※
☞ You can bake the cake the day before and make the ganache topping the following day. |

SWEET SHORTCRUST PASTRY

➺ **ENOUGH FOR A TART TO SERVE 8** • PREPARATION: 10 MINUTES • RESTING: 1 HOUR ➺

250 g (8 oz) plain flour
125 g (4 oz) butter at room temperature, cubed
2 egg yolks

75 g (3 oz) caster sugar
1 pinch of salt
grated rind of 1 unwaxed lemon
2 tablespoons marsala (or water)

PASTRY IN THE FOOD-PROCESSOR:
Put the flour and cold butter into the bowl and whiz for 10 seconds. Add the remaining ingredients and whiz again for 30 seconds. Form into a ball.

1 2
3 4

1	Sift the flour onto a pastry board and use your fingertips to rub in the butter to form breadcrumbs.	2	Make a well in the centre and drop in the egg yolks, sugar, salt, lemon rind and marsala.
3	Mix everything together with your fingertips, bringing together all the crumbs without overworking the dough.	4	Form into a ball then flatten to a thickness of about 3 cm (a good inch). Wrap in cling film and place in the fridge to rest for 1 hour.

RICOTTA, PINE NUT & RAISIN TART

➤ **SERVES 8** • PREPARATION: 30 MINUTES • COOKING: 1 HOUR ◄

50 g (2 oz) raisins
1 sweet shortcrust pastry (see recipe 77)
500 g (1 lb) ricotta
50 g (2 oz) pine nuts
2 eggs

40 g (1½ oz) melted butter
150 g (5 oz) sugar
½ level teaspoon cinnamon
grated rind of 1 unwaxed lemon
50 ml (2 fl oz) marsala

IN ADVANCE:
Soak the raisins for 10 minutes in a bowl of warm water. Drain, then sprinkle them with a little flour.

1 2
3 4

1	Work the rested dough for 30 seconds then roll out on a lightly floured pastry board.	2	Butter and flour a tart tin then line with the pastry. Prick the base with a fork and return to the fridge to rest.
3	Mix the ricotta until smooth then add all the remaining ingredients including the soaked raisins. Stir to combine.	4	Pour the mixture into the lined tin. Use your fingers to press down the sides of the pastry to meet the level of the filling. ➤

| 5 | Cook in a preheated oven at 160°C (325°F), Gas Mark 3 for 1 hour. If the surface is becoming brown too quickly, cover with aluminium foil. | **VARIATIONS**
❋

Flavour the tart with the finely grated rind of 1 unwaxed orange and make the pastry with orange water instead of marsala. You can add to the filling a little preserved ginger or candied lemon and orange rind. |

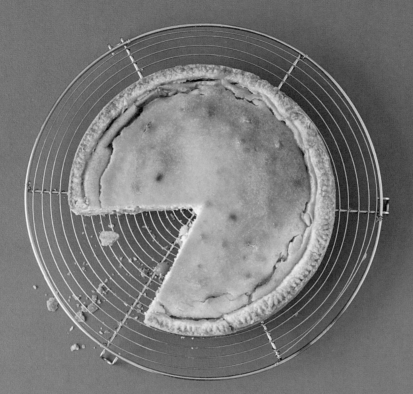

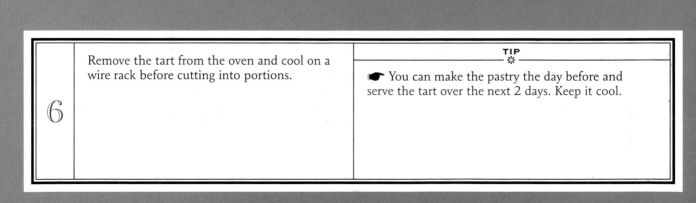

6 | Remove the tart from the oven and cool on a wire rack before cutting into portions.

TIP
❧

☛ You can make the pastry the day before and serve the tart over the next 2 days. Keep it cool.

RED FRUIT TARTLETS

⇝ **MAKES 25–30 TARTLETS** • PREPARATION: 20 MINUTES • COOKING: 15 MINUTES ⇜

1 sweet shortcrust pastry (see recipe 77)
150 g (5 oz) mascarpone
200 g (7 oz) ricotta
40 g (1½ oz) icing sugar

1 sachet vanilla sugar
grated rind of 1 lemon
2 tablespoons sweet wine
½ punnet raspberries

½ punnet strawberries
2 handfuls of cherries, pitted
IN ADVANCE:
Preheat the oven to 180°C (350°F),
Gas Mark 4.

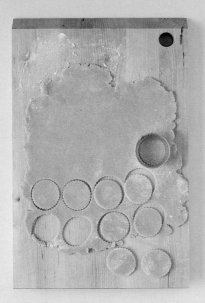

1 2
3 4

1	Thinly roll out the pastry on a lightly floured pastry board. Use a floured 10-cm (4-in) pastry cutter to cut out 25–30 discs.	2	Transfer the pastry discs to a baking sheet covered in baking paper. Prick the pastry with a fork.	
3	Cook in the preheated oven until the pastry is golden (about 15 minutes). Transfer to a wire rack and leave to cool.	4	Put the mascarpone and the ricotta in a bowl with the sugars, lemon rind and sweet wine. Work smooth with a spoon.	➤

| 5 | Spread a small teaspoonful of the cream mixture on each pastry disk then top with a whole raspberry, pieces of strawberry and the pitted cherries. | **TIP** ❀

You can make and bake the pastry disks in advance and decorate them with the cream and the fruits just before you are ready to serve. |

| 6 | It's ready! | **VARIATION**

This pastry is enough to make 1 large tart (20–22 cm/8–9 in). For the filling you need to use 250 g (8 oz) of mascarpone, 250 g (8 oz) of ricotta and 50 g (2 oz) icing sugar. |

AUNTIE'S RICE CAKE

❧ **SERVES 8–10** • **PREPARATION: 20 MINUTES** • **COOKING: 55 MINUTES** ❧

1 litre (1¾ pints) whole milk
1 pinch of salt
150 g (5 oz) risotto rice (carnaroli
or arborio)

150 g (5 oz) icing sugar + 1 tablespoon
grated rind of 1 unwaxed lemon
6 tablespoons marsala
3 eggs

IN ADVANCE:
Preheat the oven to 180°C (350°F),
Gas Mark 4. Butter and flour a large
ovenproof dish or baking tray.

1 2
3 4

1	Put the milk and the salt in a large saucepan and bring to the boil.	2	Tip in the rice and stir with a wooden spoon. Cook over a gentle heat for 8 minutes (the rice should remain al dente).	
3	Leave to cool, stirring from time to time (if you transfer it to a bowl, it will cool faster).	4	Once the rice has cooled, add the 150 g (5 oz) sugar, the lemon rind and 4 tablespoons of the marsala.	➤

5 6
7 8

5	Separate the eggs and add the yolks to the rice, one at a time, incorporating with a whisk.	6	Lightly beat the egg whites with a fork and incorporate into the rice mixture.
7	Drain the rice through a colander over a bowl, reserving the liquid.	8	Fill the prepared dish or tray with the drained rice, then pour the reserved liquid on top: this way the rice settles in the bottom of the dish and a light crust forms on the surface. Transfer the dish to the oven and bake for 45 minutes.

9 When cooked, remove from the oven and sprinkle with the extra tablespoon of icing sugar and the remaining 2 tablespoons of marsala. Serve the rice warm or at room temperature, either cut into squares or large spoonfuls.

VARIATION
※

☛ Instead of flouring the dish, you can sprinkle it with a coating of crushed amaretti over the base, rather than flour.

TIP
※

☛ The rice cake tastes even better if it can rest for 2 hours after it comes out of the oven.

BAKED PEACHES

❧ SERVES 4 • PREPARATION: 20 MINUTES • COOKING: 30 MINUTES ❧

4 perfectly ripe yellow peaches
175 g (6 oz) soft amaretti (8–10 biscuits)
1 egg yolk
1 tablespoon cocoa powder

15 g (½ oz) butter
1 small glass of sweet wine (muscat)
½ teaspoon icing sugar (optional)

IN ADVANCE:
Preheat the oven to 180°C (350°F), Gas Mark 4. Note: You can prepare this the day before, and cook it when you want to serve.

1	Cut the peaches in half (do not peel them), remove the stone then hollow out the centre slightly, reserving the flesh.	2	Blend the amaretti with the egg yolk, cocoa powder and reserved peach flesh.
3	Stuff the peach halves with the amaretti mixture. Place in a buttered gratin dish, and dot the remaining butter on the peaches. Pour over the sweet wine.	4	Cook the peaches in the preheated oven for 20 minutes. Baste them with the juices once or twice as they cook. Serve warm or at room temperature.

RICH PANDORO DESSERT

⇴ MAKES 14 SLICES • PREPARATION: 30 MINUTES ⇴

1 pandoro (Italian sweet yeast bread)
MASCARPONE CREAM:
250 g (8 oz) mascarpone + 3 egg yolks
3 tablespoons granulated sugar
4 tablespoons marsala, amaretto, rum…)

250 ml (8 fl oz) chilled double cream
2 punnets of red berries (redcurrants, blackcurrants, raspberries)
handful of red sweets
1 tablespoon icing sugar

☛ If you want to slice the pandoro in advance, put it back in its wrapping so that it doesn't dry out, and then layer it at the last moment. You can use other spirits, such as whisky, for this dessert, too.

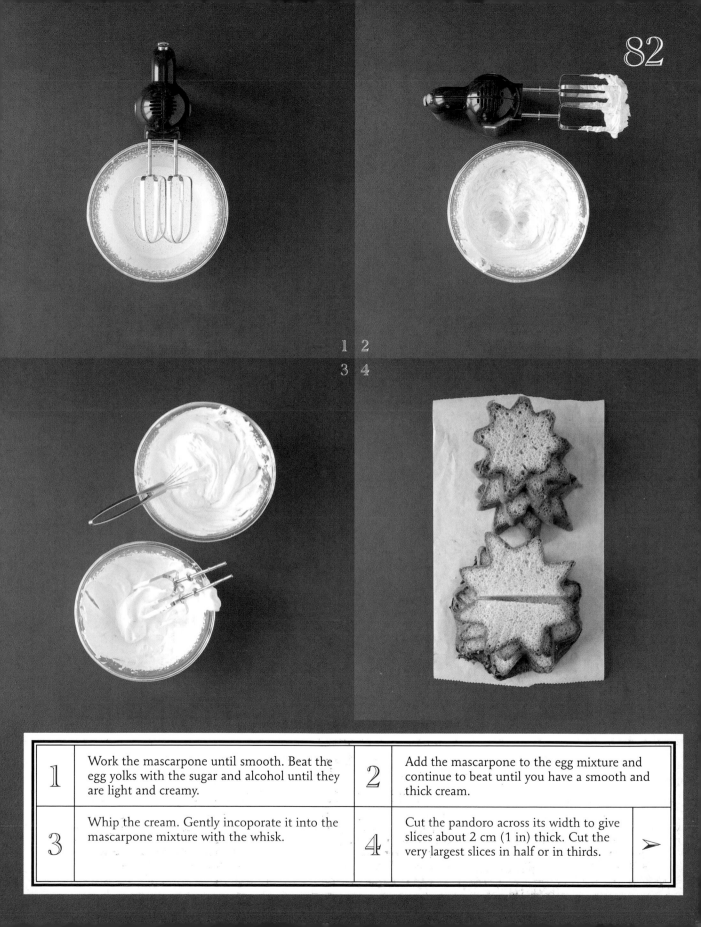

1	2		
3	4		

1	Work the mascarpone until smooth. Beat the egg yolks with the sugar and alcohol until they are light and creamy.	2	Add the mascarpone to the egg mixture and continue to beat until you have a smooth and thick cream.	
3	Whip the cream. Gently incoporate it into the mascarpone mixture with the whisk.	4	Cut the pandoro across its width to give slices about 2 cm (1 in) thick. Cut the very largest slices in half or in thirds.	➤

5	Now reassemble the pandoro on a serving plate but alternating the slices with a layer of the mascarpone cream (spread it with a spatula or pipe it on if you prefer) and fruit scattered on each layer.	**A NOTE ON PANDORO** ❋ Pandoro, along with panettone, is found throughout Italy at Christmas time. It is a sweet yeast bread, rather like brioche but star-shaped, which originated in Verona. It takes so long to prepare that all Italians buy their pandoro, provided they can find a good-quality one! Traditionally pandoro is served just as it is, with a simple dusting of icing sugar.

		TO SERVE
6	Decorate with more fruit and scatter around the red sweets. Lightly dust with icing sugar (this is provided with the pandoro), sifting it through a tea strainer.	Cut in slices and serve using a cake slicer.

APPENDICES

GLOSSARY

MENUS

TABLE OF CONTENTS

RECIPE INDEX

GENERAL INDEX

ACKNOWLEDGEMENTS

GLOSSARY

AMARETTI
Little biscuits made from bitter almonds. Amaretti di Sassello are soft while Amaretti di Saronno are crunchy.

ANCHOVIES
For preference, select the salted version when anchovies are to be cooked in a recipe and anchovies preserved in olive oil for all other dishes.

BALSAMIC VINEGAR
Look for the one from Reggio Emilia or Modena, with no additives or colouring (or a maximum of 2% caramel). See also Reduction of Balsamic Vinegar.

BARD, BARDING
This refers to stretching rashers of bacon, or cured or fatty ham, over meat or poultry to prevent it drying out during cooking.

BASIL
The quintessential Italian herb, and a staple ingredient in tomato sauces for pasta and, of course, in classic pesto.

BLACK OLIVES
When possible, look for the Italian variety called taggiasca (pronounced tadgiaska). Similar varieties are those from Gaeta or Lucca, otherwise you can use the small black French olives produced around Nice.

BORLOTTI
A pinkish-brown bean that is essential for a good bean soup. They are usually sold dried and in tins but in season you can find fresh borlotti in their pods.

BOTARGO (OR POUTARGUE)
This luxury ingredient is made from the dried eggs of grey mullet, preserved with either beeswax or paraffin wax. It is grated or shaved over a dish. Botargo made from tuna eggs has a stronger taste and a more pronounced iodine flavour.

BREADCRUMBS
These recipes use homemade breadcrumbs, made from stale bread reduced to crumbs in a food-processor.

BRESAOLA
This is air-dried, salt-cured beef. It is sold thinly sliced; look for it in good supermarkets and delicatessens.

BURRATA
A fresh cheese made from mozzarella and cream. It is very delicate and should be eaten within 3 days. Serve it as it is, or with pasta dishes.

CAPERS
Try to select salted capers which have real flavour. The best are from Pantelleria, Salina or Lipari. Rinse under cold running water to remove the salt.

CAPRINO
A fresh goat's cheese made with whole or skimmed milk from the Piedmont region of north Italy.

CARPACCIO
'Carpacchio' refers to a dish of beef (traditionally) sliced wafer thin. The dish was created by the owner of the legendary Harry's Bar in Venice, Giuseppe Cipriani, in the 1960s. He named the dish after the Venetian painter Carpaccio who used a particular red in his works that reminded Cipriani of this meat. These days the term carpaccio is used to refer to any dish that is served in extremely thin slices.

COTECHINO
This is a soft cured salami from the north of Italy made from the chopped pork meat, fat and rind. It is sold ready-cooked in vacuum packs. It is served in a traditional dish at Christmas, with lentils and mashed potato.

CRESPELLES
Crespelles are the Italian equivalent of savoury crêpes or little pancakes. They can be used instead of lasagne sheets, rolled like cannelloni, folded in half-moon shapes or tied as little pouches.

CURED HAM
Prosciutto is the generic name for Italian air-dried ham. Price tends to reflect quality. Opt for either Parma ham or one from San Daniele, sliced very thinly.

DRY, DRYING
To dry cooked spinach thoroughly, put it in a frying pan over a low heat until all the water has evaporated.

EGG PASTA
Unless you can make this yourself, opt for a good-quality (usually described as 'artisan') dried pasta.

GARLIC
Never be without garlic in your kitchen! It is used in countless dishes to flavour oil before sautéing vegetables (and usually removed once the vegetables are cooked).

GREEN OLIVES
Select the fat ones from Cerignola or Lucca or the smaller variety known as picholines.

GORGONZOLA
A blue-veined cheese that can be firm or buttery. It has a salty flavour and plenty of bite. Gorgonzola is very good as it is, with celery. Melted with a little milk or cream it makes an excellent sauce for pasta or gnocchi.

HARD WHEAT PASTA
As with any pasta, 'artisan-made' has the best flavour and texture. Allow 1 litre (1¾ pints) of water for every 100 g (3½ oz) of pasta and 10 g (½ oz) of salt. Follow the instructions for cooking the pasta until just al dente.

LARDO DI COLONNATA
This is the most famous of Italian 'lard', meaning cured pork fat, from Tuscany. It spends 6 months in marble vats, layered with herbs and spices, to develop flavour.

MARINADE
For Italians, a marinade usually means olive oil, lemon juice and herbs. Marinating meat or fish imparts flavour and helps to tenderize the flesh.

MASCARPONE
Thick Italian cream made from crème fraîche, to which buttermilk may be added. It is an essential ingredient of tiramisu, and can be used instead of butter in risotto.

MOSTARDA
A condiment from north Italy made from candied fruit spiced with powdered mustard seed or mustard essence. The most widely available is Mostarda di Cremona.

MOZZARELLA
A white cheese made from either cow's or buffalo's milk (the latter is preferable as it has more flavour). It is usually sold in its own whey or in brine, sometimes vacuum packed. Due to its high water content, it should be used quickly once opened. Serve at room temperature.

OLIVE OIL
Try to buy extra virgin, cold pressed Italian olive oil from the first pressing. As a guide, olive oils from the north of Italy are quite mild, those from the centre and the south are more fruity.

OREGANO
Another quintessentially Italian herb. Use the dried variety from southern Italy, preferably organic.

PANCETTA
Rolled dried belly of pork, smoked or unsmoked. It can be used to bard meat, or cubed and added to pasta dishes.

PECORINO ROMANO
A sheep's milk cheese which has a distinctive black rind. It is ideal for grating over pasta dishes.

PEPPER
Use freshly ground good-quality peppercorns, added sparingly and usually at the end of cooking.

PINE NUTS
Pine nuts are typical of many southern Italian dishes. The flavour is much enhanced by toasting them first.

PROVOLA (OR SCAMORZA)
A cow's milk cheese which, like mozzarella, has a stringy texture. It is found plain and, for preference, smoked.

REDUCTION OF BALSAMIC VINEGAR
This is balsamic vinegar reduced over a gentle heat to a syrup. You can buy it ready prepared (sold as 'cream of balsamic') or make it yourself (see recipe 62). It is much used for drizzling over dishes as a garnish and gives a delicious sweet-sour flavour.

RICOTTA
Ricotta means 're-cooked'. This cheese is made from the whey of cow's or, more often, sheep's milk. It is much used in Italian cooking, in savoury and sweet recipes.

SPECK
A smoked cured mountain ham, often juniper-flavoured.

STOCK
If you don't have time to make your own vegetable- or meat-based stock, make sure you buy good-quality stock cubes, preferably organic.

SUGAR
For desserts, use unrefined cane sugar.

TALEGGIO
A cow's milk cheese from Lombardy. Serve as it is or melted on bruschetta or over risotto, etc.

TINNED OR PRESERVED TUNA
Choose tuna preserved in oil for flavour. Excellent on little toasts, in salads, pasta, etc.

YEAST
For bread or pizza dough you can buy fresh yeast from a baker. Allow 25 g (1oz) fresh yeast for every 500 g (1 lb) of flour. Otherwise, buy sachets of dried yeast and follow the instructions for reconstituting it.

MENUS

A formal Italian dinner comprises an aperitif, a starter, a first course (pasta, rice, soup), a second course (meat or fish) and a dessert. For everyday meals, though, a starter and either a first or second course is more usual. In any case, pasta is always present: the reigning monarch at the table!

EXPRESS MENU

Crostini 06

Pasta + various sauces 40, 41, 42
Penne with aubergines 44
Spaghetti carbonara (without artichokes) 43

Fillet of beef 64
Saltimbocca 66
Baked marinated sea bream 59
Sicilian-style swordfish 58

Sabayon 74
Baked peaches 81

MENU FOR TWO

Salad of raw artichokes 21

Tagliatelle with mushrooms 34
Linguine with clams 46
Saltimbocca 66
Baked sea bass with fennel 61
Sicilian-style swordfish 58

Panna cotta 73
Semifreddo 75

SIMPLE AUTUMN MENU

Crostino with lardo de Colonnata 06

Borlotti bean soup 31
Papardelle with duck sauce 33
Saffron risotto 51

Milan-style osso buco 69
Veal stew with polenta 70

Chocolate amaretti cake 76
Tiramisu 72

PICNIC MENU

Sicilian-style pasta salad 48
Bread salad (panzanella) 20

Milan-style veal escalopes 65

Sicilian aubergines (caponata) 23
Tomato gratin 25

Baked peaches 81

SUMMER MENU

Bruschetta with tomato 05
Grilled peppers 16
Courgette frittata 28
Stuffed sardines 60

Vegetable stuffed pasta 49
Sicilian-style pasta salad 48
Pasta salad with Sicilian-style pesto 02
Bucatini with sardines 45

Orange & fennel salad 19
Carpaccio of octopus 57
Veal in tuna sauce 63

Tomato gratin 25
Sicilian aubergines (caponata) 23
Neapolitan-style aubergines 24
Stewed peppers (peperonata) 22

Panna cotta 73
Baked peaches 81

WINTER BUFFET MENU

Lingue with pistachio pesto 09
Mini focaccia with olives 11
Breadsticks with lardo de Colonnata & hams .. 10

Borlotti bean soup 31
Lasagne verde bolognaise 36
Risotto 50

Veal stew with polenta 70
Chicken & ricotta parcel 67

Oven-baked vegetable medley 27

Tiramisu 72
Chocolate amaretti cake......................... 76
Panna cotta 73

MENU FOR THE IN-LAWS

Lingue with artichoke pesto 09
Mini portions of herb & vegetable pie 29

Asparagus & pea lasagne 37
Spinach & ricotta crêpes 38
Ravioli stuffed with squash...................... 39

Baked sea bass with fennel 61
Guineafowl in pepper sauce 68

Semifreddo 75
Tiramisu 72

CHRISTMAS EVE

Crostini with botargo 06
Lingue with pistachio pesto 09
Mini portions of herb & vegetable pie 29

Carpaccio of octopus on rocket.................. 57

Risotto 50
Spinach & ricotta crêpes 38
Linguine with clams 46

Baked sea bass with fennel 61

Rich pandoro dessert 82
Sabayon 74
Semifreddo...................................... 75

BIG MATCH MENU

Pizza (made in advance and
subsequently reheated) 12, 13, 14
Mini fried calzone (deep-fry at half-time) 15

Tiramisu 72
Semifreddo 75

GIRLS' NIGHT IN

Raw artichoke salad............................. 21
Carpaccio (octopus or beef)............... 57 or 62
Panna cotta 73

CHILD'S BIRTHDAY MENU

Breadsticks with ham 10
Focaccia stuffed with cheese & ham 11
Pizza margarita.................................. 13

Panna cotta 73
Auntie's rice cake 80
Chocolate amaretti cake......................... 76

CHILDREN'S PARTY!

Herb & vegetable pie 29

Potato or Roman-style gnocchi .... 55 or 56
Pasta gratin 47
Chicken & ricotta parcel......................... 67

Oven-baked vegetable medley 27

Panna cotta 73

TABLE OF CONTENTS

1

STARTERS

PESTOS

Classic pesto 01
Sicilian-style pesto 02
Pistachio pesto 03
Artichoke pesto 04

TOASTED

Bruschetta with tomato 05
Bruschetta toppings: meat 06
Bruschetta toppings: cheese 06
Bruschetta toppings: fish 06
Bruschetta toppings: vegetables 06
Lingue.................................... 07
Breadsticks (grissini) 08
What to serve with lingue 09
What to serve with grissini 10

PIZZA & CO.

Focaccia with olives 11
Homemade pizza dough 12
Pizza margarita........................... 13
Pizza toppings 14
Mini fried calzone 15

2

VEGETABLES

GRILLED VEGETABLES

Grilled peppers...........................16
Grilled aubergines........................17
Grilled courgettes........................18

SALADS

Orange & fennel salad.....................19
Bread salad (panzanella)..................20
Raw artichoke salad 21

COOKED VEGETABLES

Stewed peppers (peperonata) 22
Sicilian aubergines (caponata) 23
Neapolitan-style aubergines...............24
Tomato gratin 25
Oven-baked cherry tomatoes 26
Oven-baked vegetable medley 27

LIGHT DISHES

Courgette frittata 28
Herb & vegetable pie 29
Minestrone 30
Borlotti bean soup 31

3

PASTA & CO.

EGG PASTA

Homemade pasta 32
Papardelle with duck sauce 33
Tagliatelle with mushrooms 34
Béchamel sauce 35
Lasagne verde bolognaise 36
Asparagus & pea lasagne 37
Spinach & ricotta crêpes 38
Ravioli stuffed with squash 39

SAUCES

Tomato sauce 40
Anchovy & garlic sauce 41
Chilli & bacon sauce 42

HARD WHEAT PASTA

Carbonara with artichokes 43
Penne with aubergines 44
Bucatini with sardines 45
Linguine with clams 46
Pasta gratin 47
Sicilian-style pasta salad 48
Vegetable-stuffed pasta 49

RISOTTO & GNOCCHI

Classic risotto 50
Saffron risotto 51
Mushroom risotto 52
Squash risotto 53
Leek & cotechino risotto 54
Potato gnocchi 55
Roman-style gnocchi 56

4

FISH

Carpaccio of octopus 57
Sicilian-style swordfish 58
Baked marinated sea bream 59
Stuffed sardines 60
Baked sea bass with fennel 61

5

MEAT

SLICES

Carpaccio of beef 62
Veal in tuna sauce 63
Fillet of beef 64

PAN-FRIED

Milan-style veal escalopes 65
Saltimbocca 66
Chicken & ricotta parcel 67

IN SAUCE

Guineafowl in pepper sauce 68
Milan-style osso buco 69
Veal stew with polenta 70
Polenta 71

6

DESSERTS

CREAMY

Tiramisu 72
Panna cotta 73
Sabayon 74
Semifreddo 75

CAKES & TARTS

Chocolate & amaretti cake 76
Sweet shortcrust pastry 77
Ricotta, pine nut & raisin tart 78
Red fruit tartlets 79
Auntie's rice cake 80
Baked peaches 81
Rich pandoro dessert 82

INDEX OF RECIPES

Note: This index is organized by recipe number.

A
Anchovy & garlic sauce 41
Artichoke pesto 04
Asparagus & pea lasagne 37
Auntie's rice cake 80

B
Baked marinated sea bream 59
Baked peaches 81
Baked sea bass with fennel 61
Béchamel sauce 35
Borlotti bean soup 31
Bread salad (panzanella) 20
Breadsticks (grissini) 08
    What to serve with Breadsticks 10
Bruschetta toppings 06
Bruschetta with tomato 05
Bucatini with fresh sardines 45

C
Carbonara with artichokes 43
Carpaccio of beef 62
Carpaccio of octopus 57
Chicken & ricotta parcel 67
Chilli & bacon sauce 42
Chocolate amaretti cake 76
Classic pesto 01
Classic risotto 50
Courgette frittata 28

F
Fillet of beef 64
Focaccia with olives 11

G
Grilled aubergines 17
Grilled courgettes 18
Grilled peppers 16
Guineafowl in pepper sauce 68

H
Herb & vegetable pie 29
Homemade pasta 32
Homemade pizza dough 12

L
Lasagne verde bolognaise 36
Leek & cotechino risotto 54
Lingue 07
    What to serve with Lingue 09
Linguine with clams 46

M
Milan-style osso buco 69
Milan-style veal escalopes 65
Minestrone 30

Mini fried calzone 15
Mushroom risotto 52

N
Neapolitan-style aubergines 24

O
Orange & fennel salad 19
Oven-baked cherry tomatoes 26
Oven-baked vegetable medley 27

P
Panna cotta 73
Papardelle with duck sauce 33
Pasta gratin 47
Penne with aubergines 44
Pistachio pesto 03
Pizza margarita 13
Pizza toppings 14
Polenta 71
Potato gnocchi 55

R
Ravioli stuffed with squash 39
Raw artichoke salad 21
Red fruit tartlets 79
Rich pandoro dessert 82
Ricotta, pine nut & raisin tart 78
Roman-style gnocchi 56

S
Sabayon 74
Saffron risotto 51
Saltimbocca 66
Semifreddo 75
Sicilian aubergines (caponata) 23
Sicilian-style pasta salad 48
Sicilian-style pesto 02
Sicilian-style swordfish 58
Spinach & ricotta crêpes 38
Squash risotto 53
Stewed peppers (peperonata) 22
Stuffed sardines 60
Sweet shortcrust pastry 77

T
Tagliatelle with mushrooms 34
Tiramisu 72
Tomato gratin 25
Tomato sauce 40

V
Veal in tuna sauce 63
Veal stew with polenta 70
Vegetable-stuffed pasta 49

GENERAL INDEX

Note: This index is organized by recipe number.

A

amaretti
Baked peaches 81
Chocolate amaretti cake 76
Ravioli stuffed with squash 39

anchovies
Anchovy & garlic sauce 41
Pizza toppings 14
Stuffed sardines 60

artichokes
Artichoke pesto 04
Carbonara with artichokes 43
Raw artichoke salad 21

aubergines
Grilled aubergines 17
Neapolitan-style aubergines 24
Penne with aubergines 44
Pizza toppings 14
Sicilian aubergines (caponata) 23

B

basil
Bruschetta with tomato 05
Classic pesto 01
Pizza margarita 13
Sicilian-style pesto 02
Stewed peppers (peperonata) 22

beans
Borlotti bean soup 31
Minestrone 30

béchamel sauce
Asparagus & pea lasagne 37
Béchamel sauce 35
Lasagne verde bolognaise 36

beef
Carpaccio of beef 62
Fillet of beef 64
Lasagne verde bolognaise 36

bread
Bread salad (panzanella) 20
Bruschetta toppings 06
Bruschetta with tomato 05
Milan-style veal escalopes 65

C

capers
Sicilian-style pesto 02

celery
Bread salad (panzanella) 20
Carpaccio of octopus 57

chocolate
Chocolate amaretti cake 76
Semifreddo 75

clams
Linguine with clams 46

cooked meats
Bruschetta toppings 06
Guineafowl in pepper sauce 68
Pizza toppings 14
What to serve with breadsticks 10

courgettes
Courgette frittata 28
Grilled courgettes 18

cream
Panna cotta 73
Sabayon 74
Tiramisu 72

F

fennel
Baked sea bass with fennel 61
Orange & fennel salad 19

G

gnocchi
Potato gnocchi 55
Roman-style gnocchi 56

M

mascarpone
Red fruit tartlets 79
Rich pandoro dessert 82
Tiramisu 72

mozzarella
Mini fried calzone 15

Neapolitan-style aubergines 24
Pasta gratin 47
Pizza margarita 13

mushrooms
Mushroom risotto 52
Tagliatelle with mushrooms 34

N

nougat
Semifreddo 75

O

octopus
Carpaccio of octopus 57

olives
Bread salad (panzanella) 20
Focaccia with olives 11
Sicilian-style pesto 02

oranges
Orange & fennel salad 19
Stuffed sardines 60

P

pancetta
Carbonara with artichokes 43
Chilli & bacon sauce 42

parma ham
Chicken & ricotta parcel 67
Pizza toppings 14
Saltimbocca 66

parmesan
Carpaccio of beef 62
Fillet of beef 64
Neapolitan-style aubergines 24

pasta
Asparagus & pea lasagne 37
Borlotti bean soup 31
Bucatini with fresh sardines 45
Carbonara with artichokes 43
Homemade pasta 32
Lasagne verde bolognaise 36
Papardelle with duck sauce 33

Pasta gratin 47
Penne with aubergines 44
Ravioli stuffed with squash 39
Sicilian-style pasta salad 48
Spinach & ricotta crêpes 38
Tagliatelle with mushrooms 34
Vegetable-stuffed pasta 49

peaches
Baked peaches 81

peppers
Grilled peppers 16
Stewed peppers (peperonata) 22

pizza dough
Breadsticks (grissini) 08
Focaccia with olives 11
Homemade pizza dough 12
Lingue 07
Mini fried calzone 15
Pizza margarita 13

pesto
Artichoke pesto 04
Classic pesto 01
Pistachio pesto 03
Sicilian-style pesto 02

pine nuts
Classic pesto 01
Ricotta, pine nut & raisin tart

pistachios
Pistachio pesto 03

polenta
Polenta 71
Veal stew with polenta 70

poultry
Chicken & ricotta parcel 67
Guineafowl in pepper sauce 68
Papardelle with duck sauce 33

R
red fruits

Red fruit tartlets 79
Rich pandoro dessert 82

rice
Auntie's rice cake 80
Classic risotto 50
Leek & cotechino risotto 54
Mushroom risotto 52

Saffron risotto 51
Squash risotto 53

ricotta
Spinach & ricotta crêpes 38
Pasta gratin 47
Chicken & ricotta parcel 67
Ricotta, pine nut & raisin tart 78
Red fruit tartlets 79

rocket
Carpaccio of beef 62
Pizza toppings 14
Fillet of beef 64

S
sardines
Bucatini with fresh sardines 45
Stuffed sardines 60

sauces
Anchovy & garlic sauce 41
Chilli & bacon sauce 42
Tomato sauce 40

sea bass
Baked sea bass with fennel 61

sea bream
Baked marinated sea bream 59

spinach
Herb & vegetable pie 29
Spinach & ricotta crêpes 38

squash
Ravioli stuffed with squash 39
Squash risotto 53

swiss chard
Herb & vegetable pie 29

swordfish
Orange & fennel salad 19
Sicilian-style swordfish 58

T
tarts & pies
Herb & vegetable pie 29
Red fruit tartlets 79
Ricotta, pine nut & raisin tart 78
Sweet shortcrust pastry 77

tomato sauce
Mini fried calzone 15

Pasta gratin 47
Penne with aubergines 44
Tomato sauce 40

tomatoes
Baked marinated sea bream 59
Bread salad (panzanella) 20
Bruschetta with tomato 05
Oven-baked cherry tomatoes 26
Pizza margarita 13
Pizza toppings 14
Tomato gratin 25
Tomato sauce 40

tuna
Sicilian-style pasta salad 48
Veal in tuna sauce 63

V
veal
Milan-style veal escalopes 65
Lasagne verde bolognaise 36
Milan-style osso buco 69
Saltimbocca 66
Veal stew with polenta 70
Veal in tuna sauce 63

vegetables
Asparagus & pea lasagne 37
Minestrone 30
Oven-baked vegetable medley 27
Sicilian aubergines (caponata) 23
Vegetable-stuffed pasta 49

ACKNOWLEDGEMENTS

A thousand thanks to all the team involved in this gourmet adventure:
to Pierre Javelle, for his gorgeous photography,
to my assistants: Marie Mersier (styling) and Ariadne Elisseeff (home economist),
to Audrey Génin (project management),
to the publisher Marabout and my editor Rosemarie Di Domenico,
to my friends in Vanves and my daughter Eva!
A big thank you to all those who loaned tools and equipment:
paint, cooking utensils, table settings, kitchen equipment...

For the painted backgrounds:
a big thank you to Pia Jonglez and to Céline from the boutique Ressources:
2–4 avenue du Maine, 75015 Paris, 01 42 22 58 80,
www.ressource-peintures.com

Thanks to the boutique Comptoirs de Carthage for the loan of the crockery
designed by Nelson Sepulveda (manufactured by Belart)
Comptoirs de Carthage: 27 rue de Picardie, 75003 Paris, 01 48 04 37 37
www.comptoirsdecarthage.com

ALESSI: www.alessi.com
BRANDT: www.brandt.com
DRIADE: www.driade.com
GUY DEGRENNE: www.guydegrenne.fr
HABITAT: 0800 01 08 00, www.habitat.co.uk
KENWOOD: www.kenwoodworld.com
KITCHEN BAZAAR: www.kitchenbazaar.com
MATHON 0 892 391 100, www.mathon.fr
MUJI: www.muji.co.uk
PEUGEOT: www.peugeot-moulins.com
PORCELAINES M.P SAMIE: www.porcelainesmpsamie.fr
RIVIERA & BAR: www.riviera-et-bar.fr
ROSENTHAL: www.rosenthal.de
THE CONRAN SHOP: www.conranshop.co.uk
VIREBENT: www.virebent.com
ZWILLING: www.zwilling.com

Props: Marie Mersier
Design: Alexandre Nicolas
English translation and adaptation: JMS Books llp
Layout: cbdesign